Diabetic Diet Cookbook for Beginners

Healthy Low-Sugar and Low-Carb Recipes with Pictures for a Balanced Lifestyle

Hunter Ramos

Author's Message

Before you start reading, I would like to thank you all and each for taking the time to read my cookbook.

It means a lot to me that out of thousands other books you've chosen mine.

In this cookbook, I tried to incorporate my experience with my knowledge and I tried my best not only to make this guide useful but also simple to read for anyone.

Each reader is my friend who is valuable to me.

TABLE OF CONTENTS

Introduction

A diabetic diet is a healthy eating plan that focuses on managing blood sugar levels for individuals with diabetes. It emphasizes controlling the intake of carbohydrates, particularly those with a high glycemic index (GI), as they can cause rapid spikes in blood sugar levels.

However, it's not just about cutting carbs. A balanced diabetic diet also emphasizes the importance of incorporating other nutrients like protein, healthy fats, fiber, vitamins, and minerals. Proteins help in stabilizing blood sugar levels by promoting satiety, while healthy fats slow down the absorption of carbohydrates, leading to a more gradual increase in blood sugar. Fiber, found in fruits, vegetables, and legumes, aids in maintaining steady blood sugar levels and supports overall digestive health.

A diabetic diet is crucial for individuals with diabetes as it helps regulate blood sugar levels, preventing complications such as heart disease and nerve damage. By controlling carbohydrate intake and emphasizing nutrient-dense foods, it supports weight management and improves insulin sensitivity. Additionally, a diabetic diet promotes overall health by providing essential vitamins, minerals, and antioxidants. Following this dietary approach can enhance quality of life for individuals with diabetes, empowering them to better manage their condition and reduce the risk of long-term complications.

In this book, you'll find a curated selection of the finest, most popular, and wonderfully satisfying recipes tailored specifically for individuals managing diabetes. Whether you're new to managing your diet or an experienced cook seeking new ideas, this cookbook will be your indispensable companion.

Benefits of the Diabetic diet

A diabetic diet offers numerous benefits for individuals managing diabetes, including:

- Blood Sugar Control. One of the primary goals of a diabetic diet is to help regulate blood sugar levels. By monitoring and controlling carbohydrate intake, individuals can prevent sudden spikes or drops in blood sugar, promoting overall stability.

- Weight Management. Many individuals with diabetes struggle with weight management, which can exacerbate their condition. A diabetic diet focuses on portion control, healthy food choices, and balanced meals, which can aid in achieving and maintaining a healthy weight.

- Prevention of Complications. Consistently high blood sugar levels can lead to various complications associated with diabetes, such as heart disease, kidney damage, nerve damage, and vision problems. Following a diabetic diet can help reduce the risk of these complications by maintaining stable blood sugar levels.

- Improved Insulin Sensitivity. Certain foods, such as those high in fiber and protein, can help improve insulin sensitivity, making it easier for the body to regulate blood sugar levels. By following a diabetic diet rich in these nutrients, individuals may require less insulin or other diabetes medications over time.

Overall, by following a well-balanced and nutritious diet tailored to their individual needs, individuals with diabetes can enjoy a higher quality of life and greater control over their condition.

What to eat?

A diabetic diet focuses on balancing nutrient intake to help manage blood sugar levels effectively. Overall, a diabetic diet emphasizes whole, minimally processed foods rich in fiber, lean protein, and healthy fats, while limiting refined carbohydrates and sugary treats. Consulting with a registered dietitian or healthcare provider can provide personalized guidance and support in managing a diabetic diet effectively.

Here's what to include in a diabetic diet:

- Complex Carbohydrates: Opt for whole grains such as brown rice, quinoa, oats, and whole wheat bread or pasta. These carbohydrates have a lower glycemic index, causing a slower rise in blood sugar compared to refined grains.
- Non-Starchy Vegetables: Load up on vegetables like leafy greens, broccoli, cauliflower, carrots, peppers, and cucumbers. These are low in carbohydrates and calories but rich in fiber, vitamins, and minerals.
- Lean Proteins: Include lean protein sources such as skinless poultry, fish, tofu, legumes (like beans and lentils), and eggs. Protein helps stabilize blood sugar levels and promotes satiety.
- Healthy Fats: Incorporate sources of healthy fats like avocados, nuts, seeds, olive oil, and fatty fish (such as salmon and mackerel). Healthy fats aid in reducing inflammation and can help improve insulin sensitivity.
- Fruits in Moderation: Choose whole fruits over fruit juices and dried fruits, as they contain fiber that slows down the absorption of sugar. Berries, apples, citrus fruits, and pears are good options, but portion control is key due to their natural sugar content.
- Dairy or Dairy Alternatives: Opt for low-fat or non-fat dairy products like milk, yogurt, and cheese. If lactose intolerant, consider fortified plant-based alternatives like almond or soy milk.

What to avoid?

On a diabetic diet, it's important to avoid certain foods and beverages that can negatively impact blood sugar levels and overall health. Here's what to avoid:

- Limit or avoid sugary snacks, desserts, candies, pastries, sodas, fruit juices, and other sweetened beverages. These can cause rapid spikes in blood sugar levels.
- Minimize consumption of refined grains like white bread, white rice, and regular pasta, as well as processed snacks and cereals. These foods can lead to sharp increases in blood sugar.
- Avoid highly processed foods that are high in unhealthy fats, sodium, and added sugars. These include fast food, fried foods, processed meats, and packaged snacks.
- Limit intake of foods high in saturated and trans fats, such as fatty cuts of meat, full-fat dairy products, butter, margarine, and commercially baked goods. These fats can increase the risk of heart disease.
- Reduce consumption of high-sodium foods like canned soups, salty snacks, processed meats, and pre-packaged meals. Excessive sodium intake can elevate blood pressure and increase the risk of cardiovascular complications.
- Limit alcohol consumption, as it can interfere with blood sugar regulation and may cause hypoglycemia (low blood sugar). If you choose to drink alcohol, do so in moderation and with food.
- Artificial Sweeteners. While some artificial sweeteners may be safe in moderation, others can still affect blood sugar levels or have other negative health effects. Consult with a healthcare professional before using artificial sweeteners.

1. Minimize the use of added sugars in recipes by using natural sweeteners like cinnamon, vanilla extract, or small amounts of honey or maple syrup. Be mindful of hidden sugars in condiments and processed foods, and opt for unsweetened alternatives when possible.

2. Enhance the flavor of your dishes with herbs, spices, and citrus zest instead of relying on salt, sugar, or high-fat sauces. Experiment with combinations like garlic, ginger, rosemary, thyme, cumin, and lemon to add depth to your meals without extra sodium or sugar.

3. Choose lean protein sources like skinless poultry, fish, tofu, legumes, and lean cuts of meat. Trim visible fat from meat and remove skin from poultry to reduce saturated fat intake.

4. Substitute refined grains with whole grains like brown rice, quinoa, barley, and whole wheat pasta or bread. Whole grains contain more fiber and nutrients, which can help stabilize blood sugar levels.

5. Pay attention to portion sizes to avoid overeating. Use smaller plates, bowls, and utensils to help control portion sizes, and aim to fill half of your plate with non-starchy vegetables, one-quarter with lean protein, and one-quarter with whole grains or starchy vegetables.

6. Opt for foods with a low glycemic index (GI), which have less impact on blood sugar levels. Examples include non-starchy vegetables, legumes, nuts, seeds, and whole grains.

7. Increase fiber intake by incorporating plenty of fruits, vegetables, legumes, and whole grains into your meals. Fiber helps slow down the absorption of sugar and promotes digestive health.

8. Choose healthier fats like olive oil, avocado oil, and nuts instead of saturated and trans fats. Use moderation when cooking with fats and oils to control calorie intake.

9. Opt for cooking methods such as baking, broiling, grilling, steaming, and sautéing with minimal oil instead of frying. These methods help retain the nutritional value of foods without adding excess fats or calories.

10. Pay close attention to food labels when shopping for ingredients. Look for products that are low in added sugars, saturated fats, and sodium. Choose items with high fiber content and minimal processing to support your dietary goals. Familiarize yourself with serving sizes and ingredient lists to make informed choices that align with your diabetic diet plan.

BREAKFAST RECIPES

INGREDIENTS

- I cup Greek yogurt
- 2 cups blueberries
- 2 mint leaves

Blueberry Smoothie

 10 mins   0 min   2

01 Put Greek yogurt and blueberries in the food processor and blend the ingredients until smooth.

02 Transfer the cooked smoothies to the serving glasses and decorate them with mint leaves.

NUTRITIONAL VALUE

162 calories, 12g protein, 26g carbohydrates, 3g fat, 4g fiber, 19g sugar.

INGREDIENTS

- I cup Greek yogurt
- 2 cups blueberries
- 2 mint leaves

Berries Muffins

 10 mins   30 min   6

01 In the mixing bowl, combine whole wheat flour with baking soda, coconut oil, egg, Erythritol, vanilla extract, and Greek yogurt.

02 When the mixture is smooth, add blueberries and carefully stir the muffin batter with the spatula.

03 Fill each muffin mold with muffin batter halfway through and bake them for 30 minutes at 375°F.

NUTRITIONAL VALUE

362 calories, 8g protein, 53g carbohydrates, 20g fat, 3g fiber, 19g sugar.

Raspberries Oatmeal

 10 mins   20 min   4

INGREDIENTS

- 1 cup rolled oats
- 1 ½ cups coconut milk
- ½ cup raspberries
- 1 egg, beaten
- 1 teaspoon vanilla extract

O1   Pour coconut milk into the saucepan. Add eggs and whisk the mixture until homogeneous.

O2   Add rolled oats and vanilla extract, then carefully stir the mixture. Cook the oatmeal for 10 minutes over medium heat.

O3   Cool the cooked meal to room temperature, transfer it into serving bowls, and top with raspberries.

NUTRITIONAL VALUE   312 calories, 7g protein, 21g carbohydrates, 24g fat, 6g fiber, 5g sugar.

Egg and Avocado Toast

 10 mins   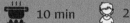 10 min   2

INGREDIENTS

- 2 whole-grain bread slices
- 1 avocado, pitted, peeled
- 2 eggs
- ¼ cup cottage cheese
- 1 teaspoon olive oil
- ¼ teaspoon chili flakes

O1   Pour olive oil into the skillet and preheat well. Crack eggs into the hot skillet and roast them for 2-3 minutes or until eggs are cooked. Sprinkle the eggs with chili flakes.

O2   Mash the avocado well with the help of the fork. Blend the cottage cheese until the texture is creamy.

O3   Toast the bread until crunchy. Spread the bread slices with cottage cheese and mashed avocado. Top the toasted bread with cooked eggs.

NUTRITIONAL VALUE   394 calories, 15g protein, 24g carbohydrates, 29g fat, 9g fiber, 3g sugar.

INGREDIENTS

- 4 eggs, beaten
- 2 bell peppers cut into wedges
- ½ tsp ground black pepper
- I tablespoon Greek yogurt
- I teaspoon olive oil

Bell Pepper Omelei

 10 mins 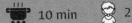 10 min 2

OI Pour the olive oil into the skillet and preheat. Add the bell pepper and cook it for 2-3 minutes on medium heat.

O2 Mix eggs with Greek yogurt and ground black pepper.

O3 Pour the egg mixture over the bell peppers and cook the omelet for 5 minutes on medium heat or until the omelet is solid.

NUTRITIONAL VALUE	262 calories, 23g protein, 15g carbohydrates, 14g fat, 2g fiber, 11g sugar.

INGREDIENTS

- 2 cups almond flour
- 4 eggs, beaten
- I tablespoon baking soda
- 2 zucchini, shredded
- I cup Cheddar cheese, shredded, I tsp garlic powder

Cheese and Zucchini Muffins

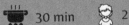 10 mins 30 min 2

OI In the mixing bowl, combine almond flour with eggs, baking powder, and garlic powder until homogeneous. Add zucchini and Cheddar cheese, then stir well.

O2 Fill each muffin mold about ¾ and bake for 30 minutes at 355°F.

O3 Allow the cooked muffins to cool down before serving.

NUTRITIONAL VALUE	532 calories, 26g protein, 17g carbohydrates, 41g fat, 8g fiber, 3g sugar.

Scramble with Avocado

 10 mins   10 min   4

INGREDIENTS

- 8 eggs, beaten
- 1 teaspoon olive oil
- 2 avocados, pitted, peeled
- 1 teaspoon ground nutmeg

01   Pour olive oil into the skillet and preheat well. Then add eggs and cook them for 1 minute.

02   Scramble the eggs with the fork until you get the desired texture. Cook the eggs for an additional minute.

03   Sprinkle the cooked scramble with ground nutmeg and transfer to the serving plate. Cut the avocados into wedges and garnish the scrambled eggs.

NUTRITIONAL VALUE   345 calories, 13g protein, 10g carbohydrates, 30g fat, 7g fiber, 2g sugar.

Kiwi and Chia Seeds Pudding

 10 mins   10 min   4

INGREDIENTS

- 2 kiwis, peeled, sliced
- 2 cups Greek yogurt
- 1 cup raspberries
- ½ cup blueberries
- ½ cup Chia seeds

01   Mix Greek yogurt with chia seeds and leave in the fridge for at least 10 minutes. Blend the raspberries in the food processor until it is smooth.

02   Fill the bottom of each serving glass with blended raspberry. Add chia yogurt.

03   Top the pudding with blueberries and kiwi.

NUTRITIONAL VALUE   195 calories, 14g protein, 22g carbohydrates, 7g fat, 9g fiber, 11g sugar.

INGREDIENTS

- 2 cups cut oats
- 4 cups water
- 1 teaspoon cinnamon
- 6 pecans, chopped
- ½ cup blueberries
- ½ cup Erythritol

Pecan Oatmeal

🕐 15 mins   🍲 10 min   👩 4

O1   Bring water to a boil and add Erythritol and cut oats and cook them for approximately 10 minutes until they are done.

O2   Sprinkle the cooked oats with ground cinnamon and stir well.

O3   Transfer the meal to the serving bowls and top with blueberries and pecans.

NUTRITIONAL VALUE	479 calories, 15g protein, 79g carbohydrates, 22g fat, 11g fiber, 22g sugar.

INGREDIENTS

- 1 ½ cups cottage cheese
- ¼ cup raisins
- ⅓ cup coconut milk
- 1 teaspoon ground cinnamon

Cottage Cheese

🕐 10 mins   🍲 0 min   👩 2

O1   Blend the cottage cheese with coconut milk until smooth.

O2   Transfer the mixture to the serving bowls and top with ground cinnamon and raisins.

NUTRITIONAL VALUE	303 calories, 25g protein, 24g carbohydrates, 13g fat, 3g fiber, 13g sugar.

Multigrain Nut Butter Toast

⏱ 10 mins   🍲 0 min   👤 2

INGREDIENTS

- 2 tablespoons peanut butter
- 2 multi-grain bread slices
- 1 teaspoon sunflower seeds

01   Mix peanut butter with sunflower seeds.

02   Spread the bread slices with the peanut butter mixture.

NUTRITIONAL VALUE

188 calories, 8g protein, 22g carbohydrates, 10g fat, 3g fiber, 4g sugar.

Low Carb Pancakes with Blackberries

⏱ 10 mins   🍲 20 min   👤 2

INGREDIENTS

- ½ cup almond flour
- 3 oz cottage cheese
- 2 eggs, beaten
- 1 teaspoon liquid stevia
- ½ teaspoon ground cinnamon
- ½ cup fresh blackberries
- 1 teaspoon olive oil

01   Mix almond flour with cottage cheese, eggs, and liquid stevia. Add ground cinnamon, olive oil, and 3 blackberries. Blend the mixture until smooth.

02   Preheat the non-stick skillet well. Pour 4 tablespoons of pancake batter into the preheated skillet and cook the pancake for 2 minutes on each side. Repeat with all remaining pancake batter.

03   Top the cooked pancakes with the remaining blackberries.

NUTRITIONAL VALUE

307 calories, 18g protein, 12g carbohydrates, 21g fat, 6g fiber, 3g sugar.

INGREDIENTS

- 4 eggs, beaten
- 1 cup fresh spinach, chopped
- 1-pound asparagus, trimmed and chopped, ½ cup cottage cheese
- 1 cup Cheddar cheese, shredded, 1 tsp black pepper, 1 tsp olive oil
- ½ cup coconut milk

Asparagus Quiche

 10 mins   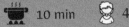 10 min   4

01 In the mixing bowl, combine eggs with spinach, cottage cheese, Cheddar cheese, ground black pepper, and coconut milk until homogeneous.

02 Brush the baking mold with olive oil well. Transfer the mixture to it. Add asparagus.

03 Preheat the oven to 375°F and cook the quiche for 30 minutes.

NUTRITIONAL VALUE	162 calories, 12g protein, 26g carbohydrates, 3g fat, 4g fiber, 19g sugar.

INGREDIENTS

- 1 cup low-fat cottage cheese
- 1/2 cup mixed fresh berries (blueberries, strawberries, raspberries)
- 2 tablespoons chopped nuts (walnuts, almonds, or pecans)
- 1 tbsp flaxseeds or chia seeds
- A drizzle of honey or a sprinkle of cinnamon

Cottage Cheese with Berries and Nuts

 5 mins   0 min   1

01 Wash the berries thoroughly. If using strawberries, hull them and cut into halves or quarters, depending on their size. Place the cottage cheese in a serving bowl. Top with the mixed berries, distributing them evenly over the cottage cheese.

02 Sprinkle the chopped nuts and flaxseeds or chia seeds over the berries. Drizzle a small amount of honey over the top or sprinkle some cinnamon for extra flavor. This step is optional; adjust according to your dietary preferences and needs.

NUTRITIONAL VALUE	250 calories, 20g protein, 18g carbohydrates, 10g fat, 4g fiber, 12g sugar.

SNACKS &
APPETIZERS

INGREDIENTS

- 4 plantains, peeled

Plantain Chips

 10 mins   15 min   4

O1   Slice the plantains with the help of the mandoline.

O2   Cover the baking sheet with the parchment and place the sliced plantains inside in one layer. Bake the plantains for 15 minutes at 350°F.

O3   Let the cooked chips cool down.

NUTRITIONAL VALUE

219 calories, 3g protein, 58g carbohydrates, 1g fat, 5g fiber, 3g sugar.

INGREDIENTS

- 2 cups strawberries
- 2 bananas, peeled, chopped
- 1 teaspoon fresh mint

Strawberry and Banana Sorbet

 10 mins   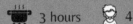 3 hours   4

O1   Put all ingredients in the food processor and blend until you get a smooth mixture. Transfer the mixture to the plastic container and freeze it at least for 3 hours.

O2   Remove the sorbet from the freezer and leave it out for around 15 minutes. Transfer the cooked sorbet to the serving bowls.

NUTRITIONAL VALUE

77 calories, 2g protein, 20g carbohydrates, 1g fat, 3g fiber, 11g sugar.

Aromatic Kale Chips

🕐 10 mins   🍲 30 min   👨 3

INGREDIENTS

- 1-pound kale leaves
- 2 teaspoons olive oil

O1 Cut the leaves in a shape you like and place them on the baking tray lined with baking paper. Flatten the kale leaves in one layer and drizzle them with olive oil.

O2 Preheat the oven to 300°F. Bake the kale leaves for 30 minutes or until the edges of the leaves become light brown.

NUTRITIONAL VALUE

75 calories, 5g protein, 16g carbohydrates, 0g fat, 3g fiber, 0g sugar.

Tomato Salsa

🕐 10 mins   🍲 0 min   👨 3

INGREDIENTS

- 1 cup Roma tomatoes, diced
- 1 chili pepper, diced
- 1 jalapeno pepper, chopped
- ¼ yellow onion, peeled, diced
- ¼ teaspoon garlic powder
- 1 teaspoon dried cilantro

O1 Put all ingredients in the food processor and blend for 1 minute.

O2 If you are not serving it right away, store it in the fridge.

NUTRITIONAL VALUE

18 calories, 1g protein, 4g carbohydrates, 0g fat, 2g fiber, 3g sugar.

19

INGREDIENTS

- 1 cup chickpeas, boiled
- 1 teaspoon curry powder
- ½ teaspoon garlic, minced
- 4 tablespoons olive oil
- 1 teaspoon lemon juice
- ⅓ cup water

Curry Hummus

🕐 10 mins   🍲 0 min   👤 4

O1 Put all ingredients in the food processor and blend until smooth.

NUTRITIONAL VALUE	305 calories, 10g protein, 31g carbohydrates, 18g fat, 9g fiber, 6g sugar.

INGREDIENTS

- 3 ripe avocados, pitted, peeled, chopped
- 4 tablespoons lemon juice
- ¼ cup fresh cilantro, chopped
- 1 Roma tomato, diced
- 1 chili pepper, chopped
- ½ garlic clove, diced

Guacamole

🕐 10 mins   🍲 10 min   👤 5

O1 Put all ingredients except the tomato in the food processor and blend until smooth. Transfer the mixture to the bowl and add tomato.

O2 Carefully mix the cooked guacamole and refrigerate it for 10 minutes.

NUTRITIONAL VALUE	259 calories, 3g protein, 13g carbohydrates, 24g fat, 9g fiber, 2g sugar.

Roasted Paprika Chickpeas

 10 mins   40 min   5

INGREDIENTS

- 1 cup chickpeas, boiled
- 1 tsp ground paprika
- ½ teaspoon salt
- 1 teaspoon olive oil

01 Preheat the oven to 400°F. Line the baking tray with baking paper.

02 Place the chickpeas on the baking tray and sprinkle with ground paprika, olive oil, and salt. Carefully mix the chickpeas and cook them in the preheated oven for 40 minutes.

03 Shake the chickpeas every 10 minutes to avoid burning.

NUTRITIONAL VALUE	156 calories, 8g protein, 25g carbohydrates, 4g fat, 7g fiber, 5g sugar.

Sweet Potato Bites

 10 mins   20 min   5

INGREDIENTS

- 3 sweet potatoes, peeled
- 1 teaspoon olive oil

01 Cut the sweet potatoes into small bites and place them on a baking sheet covered with baking paper.

02 Drizzle the olive oil over the sweet potatoes and bake them for 20 minutes at 350°F.

03 Stir the sweet potato bites gently after 10 minutes of cooking

NUTRITIONAL VALUE	10 calories, 1g fat, 1g carbohydrates, 0g fiber, 0g sugar, 0g protein.

INGREDIENTS

- 1 cup chickpeas, boiled, drained
- 2 tablespoons pesto sauce
- ¼ cup fresh basil
- 3 tablespoons olive oil
- ¼ cup water
- 2 tablespoons lemon juice

Pesto Hummus

🕐 10 mins   🍲 0 min   👤 5

O1   Put all ingredients in the food processor and blend until smooth.

O2   Transfer the cooked hummus to the serving bowl.

NUTRITIONAL VALUE	247 calories, 9g protein, 25g carbohydrates, 14g fat, 7g fiber, 5g sugar.

INGREDIENTS

- 1-pound green hulled pumpkin seeds
- 1 teaspoon ground paprika
- 1 teaspoon chili flakes
- ¼ teaspoon ground nutmeg
- 1 tablespoon olive oil

Roasted Spicy Pumpkin Seeds

🕐 10 mins   🍲 15 min   👤 4

O1   Preheat the oven to 350°F.

O2   Mix all ingredients from the list of ingredients and place them on the baking tray. Put the baking tray with pumpkin seeds in the preheated oven and bake them for 15 minutes. Stir the pumpkin seeds every 5 minutes.

O3   Let the cooked pumpkin seeds cool down.

NUTRITIONAL VALUE	544 calories, 29g protein, 14g carbohydrates, 142g fat, 4g fiber, 1g sugar.

SALAD RECIPES

INGREDIENTS

- ½ cup quinoa, cooked
- 1 cup fresh spinach, chopped
- 1 cup fresh dill, chopped
- 1 cup cherry tomatoes, halved
- ½ yellow onion, sliced
- 4 mini cucumbers, chopped
- 2 tbsp olive oil, ½ tsp black pepper, 1 tbsp lemon juice

Quinoa and Spinach Salad

 10 mins 0 min 👧 4

01 Put quinoa, spinach, dill, cherry tomatoes, onion, and cucumbers together in the salad bowl.

02 In the small bowl, mix together olive oil, ground black pepper, and lemon juice.

03 Sprinkle the oil mixture over the salad.

NUTRITIONAL VALUE — 197 calories, 7g protein, 26g carbohydrates, 9g fat, 5g fiber, 3g sugar.

INGREDIENTS

- 1 beefsteak tomato, chopped
- 2 cups fresh spinach, chopped
- ½ cup fresh parsley, chopped
- 2 bell peppers, chopped
- 1 tablespoon lemon juice
- 1 tablespoon olive oil
- 1 celery stalk, chopped

Summer Salad

 10 mins 0 min 👧 4

01 Put all ingredients in the salad bowl and carefully mix.

NUTRITIONAL VALUE — 64 calories, 2g protein, 7g carbohydrates, 4g fat, 2g fiber, 4g sugar.

Walnuts and Figs Salad

🕐 10 mins   🍲 0 min   👨 4

INGREDIENTS

- 1 cup arugula, chopped
- 1 cup spinach, chopped
- 2 figs, roughly chopped
- 2 oz walnuts, chopped
- ½ cup blueberries
- 3 oz Feta cheese, crumbled
- 2 tablespoons olive oil

O1   Put the arugula, spinach, blueberries, and walnuts in the salad bowl. Gently mix the ingredients, then add figs and Feta cheese.

O2   Sprinkle the salad with olive oil.

NUTRITIONAL VALUE

242 calories, 7g protein, 12g carbohydrates, 21g fat, 3g fiber, 8g sugar.

Cherry Tomato Salad

🕐 5 mins   🍲 0 min   👨 4

INGREDIENTS

- 3 cups cherry tomatoes
- 1 oz fresh basil, chopped
- 2 tablespoons olive oil
- ¼ teaspoon dried cilantro

O1   Roughly slice cherry tomatoes and mix them with basil, olive oil, and dried cilantro.

O2   Transfer the cooked salad to the salad bowl.

NUTRITIONAL VALUE

87 calories, 1g protein, 6g carbohydrates, 8g fat, 2g fiber, 4g sugar.

INGREDIENTS

- 1 avocado, pitted, peeled, chopped
- 1 zucchini, peeled, sliced
- 1 oz almond flakes
- 1 cup fresh spinach, roughly chopped
- 1 oz pomegranate seeds
- 1 tablespoon olive oil
- ¼ teaspoon ground black pepper

Zucchini and Pomegranate Salad

 10 mins   10 min   4

01 Mix zucchini with ground black pepper and bake at 350°F for 10 minutes.

02 In the salad bowl, combine avocado with almond flakes, spinach, pomegranate seeds, and olive oil.

03 When the zucchini is cooked, add them to the salad and gently stir.

NUTRITIONAL VALUE	192 calories, 3g protein, 9g carbohydrates, 18g fat, 5g fiber, 3g sugar.

INGREDIENTS

- 1-pound watermelon, peeled, roughly sliced
- 1 cup Mozzarella balls
- 2 cups baby spinach
- 1 teaspoon olive oil

Watermelon and Mozzarella Salad

 10 mins   7 min   4

01 Preheat the grill to 400°F and put the watermelon inside. Grill it for 3 minutes on each side.

02 Place the baby spinach in a salad bowl. Top it with grilled watermelon and Mozzarella. Sprinkle the cooked salad with olive oil.

NUTRITIONAL VALUE	149 calories, 7g protein, 9g carbohydrates, 10g fat, 1g fiber, 7g sugar.

Arugula Salad

 10 mins   10 min   4

INGREDIENTS

- ½ cup cherry tomatoes, halved, 1 tsp mustard seeds
- 2 cups fresh arugula, chopped
- 1-pound chicken fillet
- ½ tsp ground black pepper
- 1 teaspoon canola oil
- 1 teaspoon olive oil

01 Mix chicken fillet with ground black pepper and canola oil. Grill it for 5 minutes per side at 400°F.

02 Slice the grilled chicken.

03 Put the arugula and cherry tomatoes in the salad bowl. Add sliced chicken and olive oil.

04 Gently mix the salad.

NUTRITIONAL VALUE	248 calories, 34g protein, 2g carbohydrates, 11g fat, 1g fiber, 1g sugar.

Beetroot Salad

 10 mins   20 min   4

INGREDIENTS

- 1-pound beetroots
- 7 oz white cabbage
- 1 tablespoon olive oil
- ¼ tsp black pepper
- 3 cups water

01 Put beetroots and cabbage in the water and boil the vegetables for 20 minutes or until they are soft.

02 Shred the cabbage and chop the peeled beetroot. Transfer them to a salad bowl.

03 Add olive oil and ground black pepper, then gently mix the salad.

NUTRITIONAL VALUE	94 calories, 3g protein, 15g carbohydrates, 4g fat, 4g fiber, 11g sugar.

INGREDIENTS

- 1 tablespoon lemon juice
- 1 tablespoon olive oil
- 1 cup spinach, chopped
- 1 cup lettuce, chopped
- 2 cups radish, sliced

Radish Salad

🕐 10 mins   🍲 0 min   👤 4

01 Put all ingredients in the mixing bowl and carefully combine.

NUTRITIONAL VALUE	45 calories, 1g protein, 3g carbohydrates, 4g fat, 2g fiber, 2g sugar.

INGREDIENTS

- 2 cups carrot, cut into wedges
- 2 cups radish, cut into wedges
- 1 cup purple cabbage, shredded
- 2 cups lettuce, chopped
- 1 tablespoon olive oil
- ¼ teaspoon ground nutmeg
- 1 teaspoon lemon juice

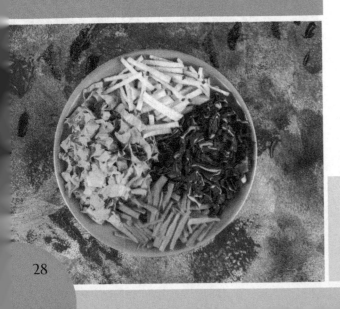

Veggie Salad

🕐 10 mins   🍲 0 min   👤 4

01 Put carrots, radishes, cabbage, and lettuce together in the salad bowl.

02 Mix olive oil, ground nutmeg, and lime juice. Pour the oil mixture over the salad.

NUTRITIONAL VALUE	72 calories, 1g protein, 10g carbohydrates, 4g fat, 3g fiber, 5g sugar.

Garden Salad

 10 mins 0 min 4

INGREDIENTS

- ½ cup Mozzarella balls
- 1 beefsteak tomato, chopped
- 2 English cucumbers, sliced
- ¼ cup black olives, pitted
- 3 basil leaves
- 1 cup fresh dill, chopped
- 1 tablespoon olive oil
- ½ teaspoon salt

O1   Put all ingredients except basil in the mixing bowl and carefully combine.

O2   Top the salad with basil leaves.

NUTRITIONAL VALUE	200 calories, 10g protein, 14g carbohydrates, 14g fat, 3g fiber, 4g sugar.

Cucumber Salad

 10 mins 0 min 4

INGREDIENTS

- 2 cucumbers, sliced
- ¼ tsp black pepper
- 1 tablespoon canola oil
- 1 tsp apple cider vinegar

O1   Put all ingredients in the salad bowl and carefully mix.

NUTRITIONAL VALUE	55 calories, 1g protein, 6g carbohydrates, 4g fat, 1g fiber, 3g sugar.

INGREDIENTS

- 1 avocado, peeled, pitted, chopped
- 1 beefsteak tomato, chopped
- 2 cups chickpeas, boiled, drained
- 2 tablespoons lemon juice
- 1 tablespoon olive oil
- 3 mini cucumbers, chopped

Avocado and Chickpea Salad

🕐 10 mins   🍲 0 min   👤 4

O1   In the food processor, blend lemon juice, olive oil, and avocado until smooth.

O2   Mix the avocado mixture with tomato, chickpeas, and cucumbers.

NUTRITIONAL VALUE	513 calories, 21g protein, 68g carbohydrates, 20g fat, 22g fiber, 13g sugar.

INGREDIENTS

- 2 cups lettuce, roughly chopped, 3 eggs, peeled, cut into wedges
- 1 cup cherry tomatoes, halved
- 6 oz tuna, canned, drained, flaked, ½ cup green beans, boiled
- ½ cup curly parsley, chopped
- 1 tbsp lemon juice, 2 tbsp olive oil, 1 bell pepper, cut into wedges

Tuna Salad

🕐 10 mins   🍲 0 min   👤 4

O1   In the mixing bowl, combine together lettuce, cherry tomatoes, bell pepper, tuna, green beans, and parsley.

O2   Add lemon juice and olive oil, then carefully stir the salad. Transfer the salad to the salad bowl and top with eggs.

NUTRITIONAL VALUE	214 calories, 17g protein, 6g carbohydrates, 14g fat, 2g fiber, 4g sugar.

GRAINS, BEANS & RICE RECIPES

INGREDIENTS

- 1 cup brown rice
- 2 cups water
- 1 carrot, diced
- 1 cup cremini mushrooms, chopped
- 1 tablespoon olive oil
- 1 teaspoon salt

Brown Rice with Pumpkin and Carrot

 10 mins    45 min   4

01 Pour olive oil into the pan and preheat it. Add cremini mushrooms, carrot, and salt, then stir the ingredients well. Cook them for 5 minutes on medium heat.

02 Add brown rice and water, stir the ingredients gently, and cover the pan with the lid. Cook the meal on medium-low heat for 40 minutes.

03 Garnish the cooked rice with kale leaves if desired.

NUTRITIONAL VALUE	214 calories, 4g protein, 39g carbohydrates, 5g fat, 2g fiber, 2g sugar.

INGREDIENTS

- 1 tablespoon coconut oil
- 1 cup hot water
- 1 ½ cup yellow couscous
- 1 teaspoon salt
- ¼ cup green sprouts

Aromatic Couscous

 10 mins   10 min   4

01 In the big bowl, mix together hot water with yellow couscous, and salt.

02 When the mixture is homogeneous, cover it and let the couscous absorb the water for 10 minutes.

03 Add coconut oil and mix well.

04 Transfer the cooked couscous to the bowls and sprinkle with greens sprouts.

NUTRITIONAL VALUE	100 calories, 3g protein, 15g carbohydrates, 4g fat, 1g fiber, 1g sugar.

Bulgur Bowl

🕐 10 mins   🍲 20 min   👤 4

INGREDIENTS

- 2 cups bulgur
- 2 cups water
- 1 beefsteak tomato, chopped, 1 tbsp olive oil
- ½ cup fresh parsley, chopped, 1 teaspoon salt

O1   Pour olive oil into the pan and preheat it. Add tomato and roast it for 3 minutes. Stir the tomato and add parsley. Cook the ingredients for 2 minutes more.

O2   Add bulgur and stir ingredients well. Add water and salt. Cover the pan with the lid and cook the meal for 15 minutes or until all liquid is absorbed.

O3   Stir the bulgur one more time and transfer it to the serving bowls.

NUTRITIONAL VALUE

279 calories, 9g protein, 55g carbohydrates, 5g fat, 13g fiber, 2g sugar.

Lentils Balls

🕐 10 mins   🍲 15 min   👤 4

INGREDIENTS

- 1 cup brown lentils, canned, drained
- 1 tablespoon all-purpose flour
- 1 garlic clove, minced
- 1 small yellow onion, peeled, minced
- 1 teaspoon dried thyme
- 2 tablespoons olive oil
- 2 tablespoons tomato paste
- ½ teaspoon salt

O1   Put brown lentils in the mixing bowl. Add all-purpose flour, garlic clove, yellow onion, dried thyme, salt, and tomato paste.

O2   Mash the mixture with your hands gently and then stir until homogeneous. Form the balls from the lentil mixture.

O3   Pour olive oil into the skillet and preheat well. Place the lentil balls in the hot oil and roast them for 4 minutes on each side.

NUTRITIONAL VALUE

107 calories, 3g protein, 9g carbohydrates, 8g fat, 2g fiber, 2g sugar.

INGREDIENTS

- 1 cup fine bulgur, ½ cup hot water, 1 tsp chili flakes, 1 tsp black pepper
- ½ tsp salt, 1 tsp coriander
- 1 tsp garlic, peeled, minced
- 1 tbsp onion, peeled, minced
- 3 tbsp lemon juice, 3 tbsp olive oil, 2 tbsp tomato paste
- 1 cup lettuce leaves

Bulgur Fingers

 10 mins 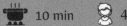 10 min 4

O1 Mix fine bulgur with water and leave it covered for 10 minutes. Then transfer the bulgur to the food processor.

O2 Add chili flakes, ground black pepper, salt, ground coriander, minced garlic, minced onion, lemon juice, olive oil, and tomato paste.

O3 Blend the mixture until smooth and homogeneous. Form the "fingers" from the bulgur mixture with your hands.

O4 Garnish the cooked bulgur fingers with lettuce leaves.

NUTRITIONAL VALUE

143 calories, 2g protein, 12g carbohydrates, 11g fat, 3g fiber, 2g sugar.

INGREDIENTS

- 1 cup cremini mushrooms
- 1 teaspoon ground peppercorns
- 2 tablespoons coconut oil
- 1 cup buckwheat
- 2 cups water
- 1 teaspoon salt
- 1 oz fresh parsley, chopped

Mushrooms and Buckwheat Bowl

 10 mins 15 min 4

O1 Put coconut oil in the saucepan and melt it. Add cremini mushrooms and salt and roast them for 5 minutes on medium heat.

O2 Add buckwheat, water, and parsley. Stir the ingredients gently.

O3 Cover the saucepan with the lid and cook the meal on medium heat for 15 minutes or until all the liquid is absorbed.

NUTRITIONAL VALUE

213 calories, 6g protein, 32g carbohydrates, 8g fat, 5g fiber, 1g sugar.

Cilantro Buckwheat

🕐 10 mins   🍲 20 min   👤 4

INGREDIENTS

- 1 tbsp dried cilantro
- 2 cups buckwheat
- 4 cups water
- 1 teaspoon salt
- 1 tablespoon butter

O1   Mix buckwheat with salt, water, and dried cilantro and boil for 20 minutes on medium-low heat or until the water is absorbed.

O2   Add butter and stir the ingredients well.

O3   Transfer the cooked meal to the serving bowls.

NUTRITIONAL VALUE

318 calories, 11g protein, 61g carbohydrates, 6g fat, 9g fiber, 0g sugar.

Brown Lentils and Carrot Bowl

🕐 10 mins   🍲 30 min   👤 4

INGREDIENTS

- 1 cup brown lentils
- 2 cups water
- ½ cup carrots, peeled, diced, 1 yellow onion, peeled, diced
- 1 bell pepper, diced
- 1 tablespoon olive oil

O1   Pour olive oil into the pan and add onion and carrot. Roast the vegetables for 5 minutes on medium-low heat, stirring occasionally.

O2   Add bell pepper, brown lentils, and water.

O3   Cover the pan with the lid and cook the meal on medium-low heat for 25 minutes.

NUTRITIONAL VALUE

80 calories, 3g protein, 10g carbohydrates, 4g fat, 2g fiber, 4g sugar.

INGREDIENTS

- 2 cups quinoa, cooked, 1 oz fresh basil leaves, 1 oz sunflower seeds
- 1 cup cherry tomatoes, halved
- 1 oz flaxseeds, 1 oz sesame seeds, 2 tbsp olive oil, 1 tbsp lemon juice, ½ tsp black pepper
- 1 oz fresh parsley, roughly chopped, 1 English cucumber, diced

Quinoa and Seeds Bowl

 10 mins   10 min   4

O1 In the shallow bowl, mix together ground black pepper, lemon juice, and olive oil.

O2 Combine quinoa, cucumber, sunflower seeds, flaxseeds, and sesame seeds. Sprinkle the quinoa mixture with the oil mixture and stir well.

O3 Garnish the cooked meal with tomatoes, basil, and parsley.

NUTRITIONAL VALUE 519 calories, 17g protein, 65g carbohydrates, 22g fat, 11g fiber, 3g sugar.

INGREDIENTS

- 1 cup brown rice
- 2 cups water
- 1 tablespoon coconut oil
- ¼ cup coconut milk
- 1 oz fresh parsley, chopped
- 1 teaspoon salt
- 1-pound cremini mushrooms, sliced

Creamy Brown Rice with Mushrooms

 10 mins   40 min 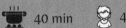 4

O1 Mix water with salt and brown rice, then cook the mixture on medium heat for 30 minutes.

O2 Melt coconut oil and add cremini mushrooms. Roast the mushrooms for 5 minutes on medium heat.

O3 Add parsley and coconut milk. Bring the mixture to a boil. Add cooked brown rice and stir the mixture well.

O4 Cook the meal for 5 additional minutes.

NUTRITIONAL VALUE 270 calories, 7g protein, 43g carbohydrates, 8g fat, 3g fiber, 3g sugar.

Coconut Meal Oatmeal with Walnuts

🕐 10 mins   🍲 20 min   👤 4

INGREDIENTS

- 2 cups cut oats
- 2 cups water
- 1 cup coconut milk
- 1 oz walnuts, chopped
- 1 tablespoon Erythritol
- 1 teaspoon vanilla extract

01   Pour water into the saucepan. Add cut oats, Erythritol, and vanilla extract.

02   Cover the dish with the lid and cook the oats for 15 minutes on medium heat. Add coconut milk, stir the mixture, and boil it for 5 minutes more.

03   When the oatmeal is cooked, transfer it to the serving bowls and sprinkle it with walnuts.

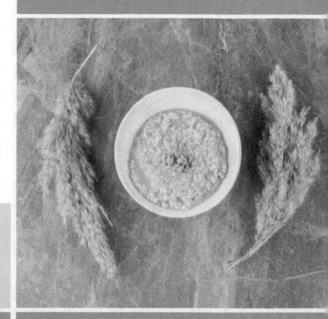

NUTRITIONAL VALUE

486 calories, 14g protein, 62g carbohydrates, 24g fat, 10g fiber, 7g sugar.

Lentils and Pumpkin Bake

🕐 10 mins   🍲 60 min   👤 4

INGREDIENTS

- 1 bay leaf
- 3 cups water
- 1 cup brown lentils
- 1 cup pumpkin, peeled, chopped
- 1 tbsp coconut oil
- 1 tsp turmeric
- 1 tsp cinnamon
- 1 apple, peeled, diced

01   Put all ingredients in the baking mold and stir gently.

02   Cover the baking mold with aluminum foil and bake the meal at 350°F for 60 minutes.

03   Remove the foil and transfer the meal to the serving bowls.

NUTRITIONAL VALUE

107 calories, 3g protein, 18g carbohydrates, 4g fat, 4g fiber, 8g sugar.

INGREDIENTS

- 1 cup black eyes beans, soaked
- 1 tablespoon curry powder
- 4 cups water
- 1 tablespoon fresh cilantro, chopped
- 1 teaspoon olive oil
- 1 yellow onion, peeled, diced

Curry Black Eyed Beans

 20 mins   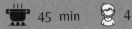 45 min   4

01 Pour olive oil into the pan and add onion. Roast the onion for 3 minutes.

02 Add cilantro and curry powder. Stir the mixture well. Add black-eyed beans and water. Stir the mixture and cover the pan with the lid.

03 Cook the meal on medium-high heat for 40 minutes.

NUTRITIONAL VALUE

93 calories, 6g protein, 14g carbohydrates, 2g fat, 5g fiber, 2g sugar.

INGREDIENTS

- 1 cup cherry tomatoes, chopped
- 1 red onion, peeled, chopped
- 2 cups white beans, boiled
- ½ teaspoon ground black pepper
- 1 cup fresh parsley, chopped
- 1 tablespoon canola oil
- 1 oz chives, chopped

Vegetables and Beans Bowl

 10 min   0 min   4

01 Mix red onion with white beans and chives.

02 Add parsley, tomatoes, canola oil, and ground black pepper.

03 Carefully stir the meal and transfer it to the serving bowl.

NUTRITIONAL VALUE

396 calories, 25g protein, 67g carbohydrates, 5g fat, 17g fiber, 5g sugar.

FISH & SEAFOOD

INGREDIENTS

- 1-pound crab meat
- 1 egg, beaten, 1 oz chives, chopped, ¼ cup almond flour
- 2 tablespoons Greek yogurt
- 1 teaspoon chili powder
- 1 bell pepper, diced
- ½ teaspoon ground black pepper
- 1 tablespoon olive oil

Crab Cakes

 10 mins   10 min   4

01 In the mixing bowl, combine chives with egg, almond flour, Greek yogurt, chili powder, bell pepper, and ground black pepper.

02 When the mixture is homogeneous, add crab meat. Stir everything well, then make the small balls from the mixture.

03 Preheat olive oil in the skillet and place the crab balls in the hot oil. Press them gently with the spatula to make the shape of cakes and roast for 3 minutes per side on medium heat.

NUTRITIONAL VALUE 176 calories, 17g protein, 6g carbohydrates, 8g fat, 1g fiber, 2g sugar.

INGREDIENTS

- 4 tilapia fillets
- 1 tablespoon olive oil
- 1 tablespoon lemon juice
- ¼ teaspoon ground coriander
- ⅓ teaspoon ground black pepper

Fragrant Tilapia

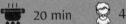 10 mins   20 min 4

01 Mix olive oil, lemon juice, ground coriander, and ground black pepper.

02 Brush each tilapia fillet with the oil mixture.

03 Place the tilapia fillets on the baking sheet and bake at 350°F for 20 minutes.

NUTRITIONAL VALUE 125 calories, 21g protein, 0g carbohydrates, 5g fat, 0g fiber, 0g sugar.

Grilled Lemony Salmon Steaks

🕐 10 mins   🍲 10 min   👤 4

INGREDIENTS

- 1 tablespoon lemon juice
- 4 salmon steaks
- ½ teaspoon chili flakes
- ½ teaspoon ground cumin
- ½ teaspoon ground paprika
- ¼ teaspoon ground black pepper

01   Mix chili flakes with ground cumin, ground paprika, and ground black pepper.

02   Rub the salmon steaks with a spice mixture, then sprinkle with lemon juice.

03   Preheat the grill to 400°F and place the salmon steaks inside the grill. Cook the fish for 4 minutes on each side.

NUTRITIONAL VALUE   239 calories, 35g protein, 0g carbohydrates, 11g fat, 0g fiber, 0g sugar.

Paprika and Orange Salmon

🕐 10 mins   🍲 25 min   👤 4

INGREDIENTS

- 1 teaspoon ground paprika
- 1 orange
- 4 salmon steaks
- 1 tablespoon olive oil
- ¼ teaspoon ground cinnamon

01   Squeeze the orange juice over the salmon steaks. Sprinkle the fish with olive oil, ground paprika, and cinnamon.

02   Gently massage the fish and put it on the baking sheet.

03   Add the squeezed orange and bake the fish at 350°F for 25 minutes.

NUTRITIONAL VALUE   290 calories, 35g protein, 6g carbohydrates, 15g fat, 1g fiber, 5g sugar.

41

INGREDIENTS

- 1-pound salmon, boiled
- 1 tablespoon dried cilantro
- 1 teaspoon ground paprika
- 1 teaspoon dried parsley
- 1 teaspoon tomato paste
- 1 egg, beaten, ¼ cup almond flour, 1 tbsp olive oil
- ¼ cup water

Cilantro and Paprika Salmon Balls

 10 mins 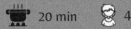 20 min   4

O1 Shred the salmon and mix it with dried cilantro, paprika, parsley, egg, and almond flour until homogeneous. Form the balls from the mixture.

O2 Preheat olive oil in the skillet well. Place the salmon balls inside and roast them for 3 minutes per side.

O3 Mix water and tomato paste. Pour liquid over the salmon balls and cover the skillet with the lid. Cook the meal for 10 minutes on low heat.

NUTRITIONAL VALUE	242 calories, 25g protein, 2g carbohydrates, 15g fat, 1g fiber, 1g sugar.

INGREDIENTS

- 1 tsp black sesame seeds
- 1 tsp sesame seeds
- 4 tuna steaks
- 1 tbsp olive oil
- ½ tsp ground black pepper

Tender Tuna Steaks

 10 mins 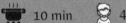 10 min   4

O1 Sprinkle the tuna steaks with olive oil and ground black pepper.

O2 Preheat the skillet well. Place the tuna steaks in the hot skillet and roast them for 4 minutes per side on medium heat.

O3 Transfer the fish to the serving plates and sprinkle with black sesame seeds and sesame seeds.

NUTRITIONAL VALUE	192 calories, 26g protein, 0g carbohydrates, 9g fat, 0g fiber, 0g sugar.

Lemony Lobster

 10 mins   15 min   4

INGREDIENTS

- 2-pounds lobster, trimmed, cut
- 1 lemon, 2 cups water

O1   Boil the lobsters in water for 15 minutes or until they become red.

O2   Squeeze the juice from the lemon.

O3   Sprinkle the cooked lobster with lemon juice.

NUTRITIONAL VALUE

208 calories, 43g protein, 1g carbohydrates, 2g fat, 0g fiber, 0g sugar.

Parmesan Lobster Tails

 10 mins   30 min   4

INGREDIENTS

- 4 lobster tails
- 4 oz Parmesan, grated
- 1 teaspoon olive oil
- 1 tablespoon Greek yogurt
- 2 cups water

O1   Boil the lobsters in water for 15 minutes.

O2   Mix Parmesan and Greek yogurt.

O3   Place the lobster tails on the baking sheet and sprinkle with olive oil. Top the lobster tails with Parmesan mixture.

O4   Bake the meal for 15 minutes at 350°F.

NUTRITIONAL VALUE

182 calories, 26g protein, 1g carbohydrates, 8g fat, 0g fiber, 1g sugar.

INGREDIENTS

- 8 whole-grain tortillas
- I cup lettuce, chopped
- I chili pepper, sliced
- I-pound shrimp
- I teaspoon olive oil
- I lime, I tsp piri piri sauce
- I tablespoon fresh cilantro, chopped

Shrimp Tacos

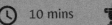 10 mins   10 min   4

O1 Mix shrimp, olive oil, and piri piri sauce.

O2 Preheat the skillet well and put the shrimp inside. Roast them for 2 minutes on each side.

O3 Mix lettuce with chili pepper, cooked shrimp, and fresh cilantro. Fill the tortillas with shrimp mixture and fold them into the shape of the tacos.

O4 Squeeze the lime juice over each taco.

NUTRITIONAL VALUE	433 calories, 31g protein, 42g carbohydrates, 17g fat, 4g fiber, 2g sugar.

INGREDIENTS

- I-pound tuna, canned, drained
- I cup Mozzarella, shredded
- 2 eggs, beaten
- I cup broccoli florets, boiled
- 2 oz Parmesan, chopped
- ⅓ cup coconut milk
- I tsp black pepper, I tsp olive oil

Broccoli and Tuna Casserole

🕐 10 mins 🍲 40 min 👤 4

O1 Brush the baking mold with olive oil.

O2 In the mixing bowl, combine tuna, Mozzarella, eggs, broccoli florets, Parmesan, coconut milk, and ground black pepper until homogeneous.

O3 Transfer the mixture to the prepared baking mold. Bake the casserole for 40 minutes at 350°F.

O4 Before serving, allow the casserole to cool well.

NUTRITIONAL VALUE	374 calories, 41g protein, 4g carbohydrates, 22g fat, 1g fiber, 2g sugar.

Grilled Thyme Shrimps

🕐 10 mins | 🍲 6 min | 👤 4

INGREDIENTS

- 2-pounds shrimp, peeled
- 1 teaspoon dried thyme
- 1 tablespoon olive oil
- 1 teaspoon lemon juice

O1 Mix shrimp with dried thyme, olive oil, and lemon juice.

O2 Preheat the grill to 400°F.

O3 Put the shrimp on the grill and roast them for 3 minutes per side.

NUTRITIONAL VALUE

301 calories, 52g protein, 4g carbohydrates, 7g fat, 0g fiber, 0g sugar.

Caldo Verde with Chorizo and Radishes

🕐 10 mins | 🍲 30 min | 👤 4

INGREDIENTS

- 4 seabass fillets
- 1 tablespoon pesto sauce
- 1 tablespoon olive oil
- 1 tsp ground black pepper

O1 Sprinkle the seabass fillets with olive oil and ground black pepper.

O2 Transfer the fish fillets to the baking sheet and bake at 350°F for 25 minutes.

O3 Top every seabass fillet with pesto sauce by making the line in the middle of each fillet and bake for 5 minutes more.

NUTRITIONAL VALUE

284 calories, 27g protein, 1g carbohydrates, 19g fat, 1g fiber, 1g sugar.

INGREDIENTS

- 4 mahi mahi fillets
- 1 tablespoon olive oil
- 1 tablespoon Greek yogurt
- 1 teaspoon ground coriander

Grilled Mahi Mahi Steaks

🕐 10 mins　　🍲 10 min　　👤 4

O1 Mix ground coriander with Greek yogurt and olive oil.

O2 Carefully brush every fish fillet with the yogurt mixture.

O3 Preheat the grill to 400°F. Place the mahi mahi fillets on the grill and cook them for 5 minutes per side.

NUTRITIONAL VALUE	124 calories, 19g protein, 0g carbohydrates, 5g fat, 0g fiber, 1g sugar.

INGREDIENTS

- 4 salmon steaks
- 1 tablespoon lemon juice
- 1 teaspoon Erythritol
- 1 teaspoon olive oil
- 1 teaspoon ground black pepper

Sweet and Sour Salmon

🕐 10 mins　　🍲 20 min　　👤 4

O1 Rub the salmon steaks with Erythritol and ground black pepper. Sprinkle the fish steaks with lemon juice and olive oil.

O2 Place the salmon steaks on the baking sheet and bake them at 355°F for 20 minutes. Flip them on another side after 10 minutes of cooking.

O3 The fish steaks are ready when they have a light brown crust.

NUTRITIONAL VALUE	163 calories, 25g protein, 4g carbohydrates, 6g fat, 0g fiber, 3g sugar.

POULTRY RECIPES

INGREDIENTS

- 1-pound chicken fillet, chopped
- 1 cup carrots, peeled, chopped
- 1 cup green peas, frozen
- 1 zucchini, chopped
- 1 cup water, 1 tbsp olive oil
- 1 tsp salt, 1 tsp black pepper

Chicken and Carrot Sauce

 10 mins 30 min 6

01 Mix chicken fillet with ground black pepper.

02 Preheat the olive oil in the saucepan well. Add chicken and roast it for 2 minutes on each side.

03 Add carrots and roast the ingredients for 4 additional minutes. Then add green peas and zucchini.

04 Sprinkle the mixture with salt and stir gently. Cook it for 4 minutes more on medium heat.

05 Add water, stir the ingredients, cover the saucepan with the lid, and cook the meal for 20 minutes over medium heat.

NUTRITIONAL VALUE — 168 calories, 24g protein, 7g carbohydrates, 8g fat, 2g fiber, 3g sugar.

INGREDIENTS

- 4 whole-grain tortilla
- 1-pound chicken fillet
- 2 bell peppers, sliced
- 1 cup lettuce leaves
- 1 tbsp olive oil, 1 tsp Greek yogurt
- ½ teaspoon ground black pepper
- 1 teaspoon ground paprika

Chicken Gyros

 10 mins 10 min 4

01 Slice the chicken fillet and mix it with olive oil, ground black pepper, and ground paprika. Preheat the skillet well and roast the chicken for 4 minutes per side on medium heat.

02 Remove the chicken from the skillet and put the tortillas inside. Cook them for 1 minute per side.

03 Spread the tortillas with Greek yogurt on one side and place the lettuce leaves on it. Add bell peppers and cooked chicken.

04 Roll the tortillas in the shape of gyros.

NUTRITIONAL VALUE — 413 calories, 39g protein, 29g carbohydrates, 16g fat, 6g fiber, 6g sugar.

Teriyaki Chicken

 10 mins 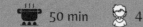 50 min   4

INGREDIENTS

- 2-pounds chicken wings
- ¼ cup diabetic-friendly teriyaki sauce
- 1 teaspoon olive oil

01 Mix chicken wings with teriyaki sauce and olive oil. Let the chicken wings marinate for 10 minutes.

02 Cover the baking sheet with aluminum foil and place the chicken wings inside in one layer. Bake the chicken wings for 50 minutes at 350°F.

NUTRITIONAL VALUE

484 calories, 70g protein, 5g carbohydrates, 19g fat, 0g fiber, 2g sugar.

Lemon and Garlic Chicken Wings

 10 mins   45 min   4

INGREDIENTS

- 1 teaspoon garlic powder
- 2-pounds chicken wings
- 1 teaspoon ground black pepper
- 2 tablespoons lemon juice
- 1 tablespoon olive oil

01 Sprinkle the chicken wings with garlic powder, ground black pepper, lemon juice, and olive oil.

02 Place the chicken wings on the baking sheet in one layer. Bake them at 355°F for 45 minutes.

NUTRITIONAL VALUE

467 calories, 66g protein, 1g carbohydrates, 20g fat, 0g fiber, 1g sugar.

INGREDIENTS

- 2 zucchini, grated
- I-pound ground chicken
- I teaspoon ground coriander
- I teaspoon salt
- ¼ cup almond flour
- I egg, beaten
- I tablespoon Greek yogurt
- ¼ cup fresh dill, chopped
- 2 oz chives, chopped

Chicken and Zucchini Pancakes

🕐 15 mins   🍲 15 min   👤 4

OI Squeeze the juice from the zucchini and put it in the mixing bowl. Add ground chicken, ground coriander, chives, dill, salt, almond flour, egg, and Greek yogurt. Combine everything until homogeneous.

O2 Preheat the non-stick skillet well. Put 2 tablespoons of chicken mixture into the skillet and flatten it into the shape of a pancake. Roast the pancake for 4 minutes per side or until the pancake is golden brown.

O3 Repeat these steps with all the mixture.

NUTRITIONAL VALUE	306 calories, 38g protein, 7g carbohydrates, 13g fat, 3g fiber, 3g sugar.

INGREDIENTS

- 2-pounds chicken wings
- I tablespoon dried oregano
- I tablespoon orange juice
- I teaspoon canola oil
- I teaspoon dried garlic

Oregano Chicken Wings

🕐 15 mins   🍲 55 min   👤 4

OI Mix chicken wings with dried oregano, orange juice, canola oil, and dried garlic.

O2 Leave the mixture to marinate for IO minutes.

O3 Place the chicken wings on the baking sheet, flatten them in one layer, and bake at 355°F for 55 minutes.

NUTRITIONAL VALUE	469 calories, 66g protein, 1g carbohydrates, 20g fat, 1g fiber, 1g sugar.

Chicken Stuffed Zucchini

🕐 20 mins   🍲 60 min   👨‍🍳 4

01   Cut the zucchini in half lengthwise and scrape seeds and flesh from it with a spoon leaving a ¼-inch border.

02   In the mixing bowl, combine ground chicken with onion, ground black pepper, salt, Tomato, and egg until homogeneous.

03   Fill the zucchini boards with ground chicken mixture and top with Parmesan.

04   Place the zucchini boats on the baking sheet and bake at 355°F for 60 minutes.

NUTRITIONAL VALUE

377 calories, 47g protein, 13g carbohydrates, 16g fat, 3g fiber, 6g sugar.

INGREDIENTS

- 4 zucchini
- 4 oz Parmesan, grated
- 1-pound ground chicken
- 1 onion, diced
- 1 tsp black pepper
- ½ teaspoon salt
- 1 Roma tomato, diced
- 1 egg, beaten

Chicken Sauie

🕐 10 mins   🍲 10 min   👨‍🍳 4

01   Pour olive oil into the saucepan and add bell peppers and chili pepper. Roast the vegetables for 3 minutes.

02   Add tomatoes, chili flakes, and ground paprika. Stir the ingredients and cook them for 7 additional minutes on medium heat.

03   Add chicken and water, stir the ingredients one more time, and cover the saucepan with the lid.

04   Cook the meal for 10 minutes over medium-low heat.

NUTRITIONAL VALUE

504 calories, 67g protein, 10g carbohydrates, 21g fat, 2g fiber, 7g sugar.

INGREDIENTS

- 3 bell peppers, chopped
- 2 beefsteak tomatoes, chopped
- 2-pounds chicken fillet, chopped, 1 cup water
- 1 teaspoon chili flakes
- 1 chili pepper, chopped
- 1 teaspoon ground paprika
- 1 tablespoon olive oil

INGREDIENTS

- 2-pounds ground chicken
- 1 teaspoon chili flakes
- 1 Roma tomato, crushed
- 1 oz fresh parsley, chopped
- 1 teaspoon olive oil
- 1 red onion, diced
- 1 garlic clove, minced
- 1 teaspoon ground black pepper
- 1 tablespoon lemon juice

Chicken Balls

 15 mins 15 min 4

01 In the mixing bowl, combine ground chicken with chili flakes, parsley, onion, garlic, ground black pepper, and lemon juice.

02 Form the medium size balls from the chicken mixture.

03 Preheat the skillet well. Place the chicken balls inside and roast them for 5 minutes on each side.

04 Add crushed tomato and stir gently. Cook the chicken balls for 2 additional minutes on low heat under the lid.

NUTRITIONAL VALUE 469 calories, 67g protein, 6g carbohydrates, 18g fat, 2g fiber, 3g sugar.

INGREDIENTS

- ½ cup almond flour
- 2 eggs, beaten
- 4 oz Parmesan, grated
- 1 teaspoon ground paprika
- ¼ teaspoon dried garlic
- ½ cup tomatoes, crushed
- 1 teaspoon olive oil
- 4 chicken fillets
- 1 oz basil leaves

Parmesan Chicken

 10 mins 40 min 4

01 Sprinkle the chicken fillets with ground paprika and dried garlic. Dip the chicken in the eggs and coat in the almond flour.

02 Preheat the olive oil well. Place the chicken in the hot oil and roast it for 3 minutes on each side.

03 Mix tomatoes and basil. Place the mixture on the baking sheet. Add roasted chicken.

04 Sprinkle the chicken with Parmesan and bake at 355°F for 30 minutes.

NUTRITIONAL VALUE 502 calories, 58g protein, 6g carbohydrates, 27g fat, 2g fiber, 1g sugar.

MEAT
RECIPES

INGREDIENTS

- 1 tablespoon quick-cooking oats, 1 yellow onion, chopped
- 1 tablespoon coconut milk
- 1-pound ground beef
- ½ teaspoon salt, ¼ cup water
- ½ teaspoon ground black pepper, 2 tbsp tomato sauce

Basil Meatloaf

 10 mins 60 min 6

O1 In the mixing bowl, combine quick-cooking oats, onion, coconut milk, ground beef, salt, water, and ground black pepper.

O2 Transfer the mixture to the non-stick baking mold. Flatten the meatloaf gently and bake at 350°F for 40 minutes.

O3 Top the meatloaf with tomato sauce and bake for 20 minutes more.

NUTRITIONAL VALUE

159 calories, 23g protein, 3g carbohydrates, 5g fat, 1g fiber, 1g sugar.

INGREDIENTS

- 2-pounds beef roast meat
- 1 tablespoon coconut oil
- 1 teaspoon ground black pepper, 1 tablespoon salt

Tender Beef Roast

 15 mins 75 min 4

O1 Rub the beef with ground black pepper, coconut oil, and salt. Wrap it in aluminum foil.

O2 Bake the beef roast meat for 75 minutes at 350°F.

O3 Discard the foil and slice the cooked meat into servings.

NUTRITIONAL VALUE

343 calories, 40g protein, 5g carbohydrates, 15g fat, 0g fiber, 0g sugar.

Tender Beef Goulash

 10 mins   30 min   4

INGREDIENTS

- 1 bay leaf, 1 tbsp tomato paste, 1 yellow onion, diced
- 2-pounds beef loin, chopped, 3 cups water
- 1 tablespoon canola oil
- 1 teaspoon peppercorns
- 1 teaspoon chili flakes
- 1 teaspoon salt

01 Pour olive oil into the saucepan and preheat well. Add onion and roast it for 3 minutes.

02 Add beef loin, peppercorns, chili flakes, and salt. Stir the meat mixture well. Cook it on medium heat for 7 minutes.

03 Add water, bay leaf, and tomato paste. Stir the ingredients until homogeneous. Cover the saucepan with the lid and cook the goulash on medium heat for 20 minutes.

NUTRITIONAL VALUE
655 calories, 73g protein, 2g carbohydrates, 38g fat, 0g fiber, 1g sugar.

Rosemary Dinner Brisket

 15 mins   14 min   4

INGREDIENTS

- 2-pounds beef brisket
- 1 tablespoon dried rosemary
- 1 teaspoon chili flakes
- 1 teaspoon salt

01 Cut the beef brisket into servings and rub with dried rosemary, chili flakes, and salt.

02 Preheat the grill to 400°F.

03 Cook the beef brisket on the grill for 7 minutes per side.

NUTRITIONAL VALUE
425 calories, 69g protein, 1g carbohydrates, 14g fat, 0g fiber, 0g sugar.

INGREDIENTS

- 1-pound beef loin, chopped
- 1 cup carrots, peeled, chopped
- 1 chili pepper, chopped
- 1 tbsp tomato paste
- 1 tsp ground black pepper
- ¼ cup cilantro, chopped
- 2 cups water
- 1 tablespoon olive oil

Beef and Carrot Stew

 15 mins 35 min 4

01 Pour olive oil into the saucepan and preheat it. Add beef loin and roast it for 5 minutes.

02 Stir the meat well and add all remaining ingredients. Stir again and cover it with the lid.

03 Cook the stew on medium-low heat for 30 minutes.

NUTRITIONAL VALUE	325 calories, 33g protein, 4g carbohydrates, 19g fat, 1g fiber, 2g sugar.

INGREDIENTS

- 4 whole-wheat pita bread
- 1 red onion, peeled, sliced
- 1 tsp sumac, 1 tsp olive oil
- ¼ cup fresh parsley, chopped
- 2-pounds beef loin, chopped
- 1 tablespoon ground paprika
- ½ tsp ground black pepper
- 1 tablespoon lemon juice

Paprika Beef Kabob

 15 mins 10 min 4

01 In the mixing bowl, combine beef loin with ground black pepper, ground paprika, and lemon juice. Marinate the meat for 10 minutes.

02 Grill the meat at 400°F for 4 minutes on each side.

03 Mix olive oil, sumac, and red onion. Put it on the pitta. Add cooked meat.

NUTRITIONAL VALUE	603 calories, 68g protein, 39g carbohydrates, 21g fat, 6g fiber, 2g sugar.

Cilantro Meatballs

🕐 15 mins 🍲 15 min 👤 4

INGREDIENTS

- ½ cup fresh cilantro, chopped
- I-pound ground beef
- I teaspoon salt, I egg, beaten, I tsp black pepper
- I yellow onion, minced
- I tablespoon olive oil

O1 In the mixing bowl, combine cilantro with ground beef, salt, egg, ground black pepper, and onion until homogeneous.

O2 Form the meatballs from the mixture.

O3 Preheat olive oil in the skillet. Place the meatballs in the hot oil and roast them for 4 minutes per side.

NUTRITIONAL VALUE

270 calories, 36g protein, 3g carbohydrates, 12g fat, 1g fiber, 1g sugar.

Grilled Pork Strips

🕐 10 mins 🍲 20 min 👤 4

INGREDIENTS

- I teaspoon sesame seeds
- I oz chives, chopped
- I-pound pork loin, sliced
- I tsp ground black pepper
- I teaspoon lemon juice
- I teaspoon olive oil
- ½ tsp ground turmeric

O1 Sprinkle the sliced pork loin with ground black pepper, lemon juice, olive oil, and ground turmeric.

O2 Preheat the grill to 400°F. Place the pork loin slices inside and roast them for 5 minutes per side.

O3 Transfer the cooked pork strips to the plate and sprinkle with sesame seeds and chives.

NUTRITIONAL VALUE

295 calories, 31g protein, 1g carbohydrates, 17g fat, 1g fiber, 0g sugar.

INGREDIENTS

- 2 oz Parmesan, grated
- 1-pound ground beef
- 1 oz fresh basil, chopped
- 1 tsp black pepper
- 4 garlic cloves, minced
- 2 beefsteak tomatoes, peeled, chopped, 1 red onion, diced
- 1 tsp dried sage, 1 tsp olive oil

Basil Meat Sauce

 15 mins 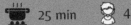 25 min 4

O1 Preheat olive oil in the skillet, then add garlic and onion. Roast the vegetables for 3 minutes.

O2 Add ground beef and roast it for 7 minutes, stirring occasionally.

O3 Add all remaining ingredients and carefully mix the mixture. Cook the dish on medium-low heat under the lid for 15 more minutes.

O4 Stir the cooked meat sauce well.

NUTRITIONAL VALUE	297 calories, 40g protein, 7g carbohydrates, 12g fat, 2g fiber, 3g sugar.

INGREDIENTS

- 1-pound beef loin, finely chopped
- 2 sweet potatoes, peeled, finely chopped
- ¼ cup fresh cilantro, chopped
- 1 tablespoon coconut oil
- 1 teaspoon ground black pepper
- ¼ cup water, ¼ teaspoon salt

Meat and Sweet Potato Bake

 10 mins 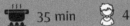 35 min 4

O1 Mix beef loin with salt and ground black pepper.

O2 Preheat the coconut oil in the skillet and place the meat inside. Roast it for 10 minutes over medium heat.

O3 Add sweet potatoes and stir well. Cook the ingredients for 5 minutes.

O4 Add water and cover the skillet with the lid. Transfer the skillet to the oven and bake the meal for 20 minutes at 350°F.

O5 When the meal is cooked, sprinkle it with fresh cilantro.

NUTRITIONAL VALUE	283 calories, 31g protein, 11g carbohydrates, 13g fat, 2g fiber, 0g sugar.

VEGETABLE RECIPES

INGREDIENTS

- ½ cup fresh cilantro, chopped
- 1 garlic clove, minced
- 1 tablespoon olive oil
- 1 teaspoon salt
- 1-pound eggplants, sliced
- 1 tablespoon canola oil

Grilled Cilantro Eggplant Coins

 10 mins   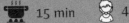 15 min   4

O1 Mix sliced eggplants with salt and leave for 10 minutes. Drain the eggplant juice and sprinkle the vegetables with canola oil.

O2 Preheat the grill to 400°F. Place the eggplant slices on the grill and cook for 4 minutes per side.

O3 Mix cilantro with garlic and olive oil. Brush the cooked eggplant coins with the cilantro mixture.

NUTRITIONAL VALUE	92 calories, 1g protein, 7g carbohydrates, 7g fat, 4g fiber, 3g sugar.

INGREDIENTS

- 4 bell peppers, chopped
- 1 red onion, peeled, chopped
- 3 beefsteak tomatoes, chopped
- 3 eggplants, peeled, chopped
- 4 garlic cloves, peeled, diced
- ¼ cup fresh cilantro, chopped
- ½ cup Italian parsley, chopped
- 2 tablespoons canola oil
- 1 teaspoon salt

Vegetable Saute

 10 mins   25 min   4

O1 Pour canola oil into the pan and preheat it. Add onion and roast it for 3 minutes.

O2 Add garlic, bell peppers, eggplants, and tomatoes. Stir the vegetables well and cook on medium heat for 20 minutes.

O3 Sprinkle the vegetable mixture with salt, cilantro, and parsley, then stir well. Cook the meal for 2 additional minutes under the lid.

NUTRITIONAL VALUE	239 calories, 7g protein, 41g carbohydrates, 8g fat, 18g fiber, 22g sugar.

Stuffed Sweet Potato

 10 mins   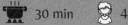 30 min   4

INGREDIENTS

- 4 sweet potatoes, halved
- ¼ cup raisins
- 1 cup Mozzarella, shredded
- 1 teaspoon olive oil

01 Place the halved sweet potatoes on the baking sheet and sprinkle with olive oil. Bake them for 20 minutes at 350°F.

02 Shred the sweet potato flesh with a fork. Top the sweet potato flesh with Mozzarella and raisins, then bake for 10 additional minutes.

NUTRITIONAL VALUE

140 calories, 7g protein, 10g carbohydrates, 9g fat, 3g fiber, 93mg cholesterol, 45mg sodium, 200mg potassium.

Mushroom Bake

 10 mins   20 min   4

INGREDIENTS

- 2 tablespoons olive oil
- 1 tsp ground black pepper
- 1 oz chives
- 3 cups cremini mushrooms, halved, 1 teaspoon salt
- ¼ cup water

01 Preheat olive oil well and add cremini mushrooms. Sprinkle them with salt, stir gently, and cook on medium heat for 10 minutes.

02 Add ground black pepper and water. Stir the mushrooms well and transfer them to the oven.

03 Bake the mushrooms at 350°F for 10 minutes. Top the cooked mushrooms with chopped chives.

NUTRITIONAL VALUE

79 calories, 2g protein, 3g carbohydrates, 7g fat, 1g fiber, 1g sugar.

INGREDIENTS

- 2-pounds Brussels sprouts, halved
- 1 teaspoon ground black pepper
- 1 tablespoon olive oil
- 1 tablespoon lemon juice

Roasted Brussels Sprouts Halves

 10 mins 15 min 4

O1 Pour olive oil into the skillet and preheat well.

O2 Sprinkle Brussels sprouts with ground black pepper. Place the Brussels sprouts in the hot oil and roast them for 4 minutes per side.

O3 Transfer the cooked Brussels sprouts to the serving plate and sprinkle them with lemon juice.

NUTRITIONAL VALUE

131 calories, 8g protein, 21g carbohydrates, 4g fat, 9g fiber, 5g sugar.

INGREDIENTS

- 8 oz cabbage leaves
- 1 cup short-grain rice, boiled
- 1 teaspoon ground black pepper
- 1 cup tomato juice
- 1 teaspoon Erythritol
- ¼ cup fresh parsley, chopped

Cabbage Rolls

 15 mins 35 min 4

O1 Mix ground black pepper with rice. Place the rice mixture on each cabbage leaf and roll them.

O2 Transfer the cabbage rolls to the baking pan.

O3 In the mixing bowl, combine tomato juice with Erythritol. Pour the tomato juice mixture over the cabbage rolls.

O4 Bake them at 350°F for 35 minutes. Top the cooked cabbage rolls with fresh parsley.

NUTRITIONAL VALUE

197 calories, 5g protein, 45g carbohydrates, 1g fat, 3g fiber, 5g sugar.

Lemony Artichoke

🕐 10 mins   🍲 10 min   👤 4

INGREDIENTS

- 1-pound artichoke, trimmed
- 2 tablespoons lemon juice
- 1 teaspoon lemon zest
- 2 tablespoons olive oil
- ¼ tsp ground black pepper
- 4 cups water

01 Bring water to a boil and put the artichoke inside. Boil the vegetables for 5 minutes over medium heat.

02 Preheat the olive oil in the skillet. Add lemon zest, lemon juice, and ground black pepper. Roast the mixture for 1 minute.

03 Drain the water from the cooked artichokes. Transfer the artichokes to the serving plate and sprinkle them with hot lemon mixture.

NUTRITIONAL VALUE

117 calories, 4g protein, 12g carbohydrates, 7g fat, 6g fiber, 1g sugar.

Spinach and Sweet Potato Bake

🕐 10 mins   🍲 40 min   👤 4

INGREDIENTS

- 2 sweet potatoes, peeled, diced
- 2 cups spinach, chopped
- 4 eggs, beaten
- 1 cup Mozzarella, shredded
- ¼ cup coconut milk
- 1 teaspoon ground black pepper
- 1 teaspoon olive oil

01 Brush the baking mold with olive oil.

02 Combine all remaining ingredients and place them in the baking mold. Flatten the mixture gently and bake at 350°F for 40 minutes or until the bake is light brown.

03 Cool the cooked meal to room temperature before serving.

NUTRITIONAL VALUE

177 calories, 9g protein, 13g carbohydrates, 11g fat, 2g fiber, 1g sugar.

INGREDIENTS

- 1 tablespoon fresh mint, chopped
- 1 avocado, pitted, peeled, sliced
- 2 beefsteak tomatoes, sliced
- 1 teaspoon flaxseeds
- 4 corn tortillas

Vegetable Quesadilla

 15 mins 0 min 4

01 Place the tomatoes and avocado on tortillas. Add fresh mint and flaxseeds.

02 Fold the tortillas into the shape of quesadillas.

NUTRITIONAL VALUE	171 calories, 3g protein, 18g carbohydrates, 11g fat, 6g fiber, 2g sugar.

INGREDIENTS

- 3 cups pumpkin, peeled, chopped
- 1 anise star
- ¼ tsp black pepper
- 4 cups water

Pumpkin Cold Soup

 15 mins 15 min 4

01 Put pumpkin and anise star in water and boil it for 15 minutes or until the pumpkin is soft.

02 Drain half of all water and remove the anise star. Transfer the pumpkin and remaining water to the food processor.

03 Blend until smooth, then add ground black pepper. Allow the soup to cool down before serving.

NUTRITIONAL VALUE	64 calories, 2g protein, 15g carbohydrates, 1g fat, 5g fiber, 6g sugar.

Tender Pumpkin Wedges

🕐 15 mins   🍲 40 min   👤 4

INGREDIENTS

- 2-pounds pumpkin, cut into wedges
- I teaspoon dried thyme
- I teaspoon ground cinnamon

O1   Rub the pumpkin wedges with ground cinnamon and dried thyme.

O2   Place the pumpkin wedges on the baking sheet and bake them for 40 minutes at 350°F or until the pumpkin is soft.

NUTRITIONAL VALUE   159 calories, 5g protein, 38g carbohydrates, 1g fat, 14g fiber, 15g sugar.

Zucchini and Nuts Spaghetti

🕐 15 mins   🍲 5 min   👤 4

INGREDIENTS

- 4 zucchini, trimmed
- ¼ cup walnuts, chopped
- I tablespoon olive oil
- I teaspoon lemon juice

O1   Make the spirals from the zucchini with the help of the spiralizer.

O2   Preheat olive oil well and put the spiralized zucchini inside. Roast it for 3 minutes stirring occasionally.

O3   Transfer the cooked zucchini to the serving plate, and sprinkle it with lemon juice, and chopped walnuts.

NUTRITIONAL VALUE   111 calories, 4g protein, 7g carbohydrates, 9g fat, 3g fiber, 4g sugar.

INGREDIENTS

- 2 pounds carrot, peeled, trimmed
- 1 teaspoon ground nutmeg
- 1 teaspoon coconut oil
- ½ teaspoon ground cinnamon
- ¼ cup water

Spiced Roasted Carrot

 15 mins   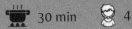 30 min   4

O1   Mix the carrot with ground nutmeg, coconut oil, and ground cinnamon.

O2   Pour water onto the baking sheet. Add carrot.

O3   Bake the carrot at 355°F for 30 minutes.

NUTRITIONAL VALUE	107 calories, 2g protein, 23g carbohydrates, 1g fat, 6g fiber, 11g sugar.

INGREDIENTS

- ¼ cup fresh parsley, chopped
- 2 cups red kidney beans, soaked
- 3 cups water
- 1 garlic clove, diced
- 1 teaspoon salt
- 1 tablespoon olive oil

Garlic & Parsley Red Kidney Beans

 10 mins   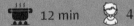 12 min   4

O1   Pour olive oil into the pan and preheat it well. Add garlic clove and roast it for 1 minute.

O2   Add red kidney beans, water, and salt. Cover the pan with the lid and cook the beans for 10 minutes.

O3   Garnish the cooked dish with chopped parsley.

NUTRITIONAL VALUE	344 calories, 21g protein, 57g carbohydrates, 5g fat, 14g fiber, 2g sugar.

DESSERTS

INGREDIENTS

- ½ cup butter, ¼ cup Erythritol, 1 egg, beaten
- 1 teaspoon vanilla extract
- 1 teaspoon baking soda
- 1 cup all-purpose flour
- 1 cup sugar-free chocolate chips

Sugar-Free Chocolate Chip Cookies

 10 mins   15 min   4

O1 Preheat oven to 350°F.

O2 Mix all ingredients until you get a homogeneous batter.

O3 Cover the baking sheet with parchment.

O4 Form the cookies with the help of the scoop and put them on the prepared baking sheet.

O5 Bake the cookies for 10 minutes.

NUTRITIONAL VALUE

359 calories, 5g protein, 47g carbohydrates, 26g fat, 2g fiber, 2g sugar.

INGREDIENTS

- ½ cup cocoa powder
- 1 cup all-purpose flour
- 1 teaspoon vanilla extract
- 1 teaspoon baking powder
- ¼ cup olive oil
- ½ cup Erythritol
- 3 eggs, beaten

Diabetic Friendly Brownie

 15 mins   30 min 4

O1 Put all ingredients in the food processor and mix until you get a smooth batter.

O2 Pour the batter into the brownie mold and flatten its surface gently. Bake the brownie at 350°F for 30 minutes.

O3 Let the cooked brownie cool down, then cut it into servings.

NUTRITIONAL VALUE

298 calories, 9g protein, 43g carbohydrates, 18g fat, 4g fiber, 13g sugar.

Apple Pie

🕐 25 mins   🍲 30 min   👤 4

01 In the mixing bowl, combine flour, butter, egg, and vanilla extract. Knead the soft dough. Cut the dough into 2 parts.

02 Mix apples with ground cinnamon and Erythritol.

03 Make the pie crust from the first part and put the apple mixture over it.

04 Roll out the remaining part of the dough and cut it into stripes. Place the stripes of the dough over the apples as shown in the picture.

05 Bake the pie at 355°F for 30 minutes.

NUTRITIONAL VALUE

324 calories, 5g protein, 60g carbohydrates, 13g fat, 5g fiber, 3g sugar.

INGREDIENTS

- 1 cup all-purpose flour
- ¼ cup butter, softened
- 1 egg, beaten
- 3 Granny Smith apples, peeled, diced, 1 tsp vanilla extract
- ¼ cup Erythritol
- 1 teaspoon ground cinnamon

Plum Tart

🕐 15 mins   🍲 45 min   👤 4

01 Mix butter with flour, baking soda, and vanilla extract. Knead the dough. Then cut it into 2 even parts and make the pie crust from one part of the dough.

02 Put the plums over the pie crust. Sprinkle them with Erythritol.

03 Roll out the second part of the dough and cut it into stripes. Place the stripes over the plums and bake the tart at 350°F for 35 minutes.

04 Cool the cooked tart well.

NUTRITIONAL VALUE

227 calories, 4g protein, 45g carbohydrates, 12g fat, 1g fiber, 21g sugar.

INGREDIENTS

- 1 cup all-purpose flour
- ¼ cup butter, softened
- 1 teaspoon baking soda
- 1 teaspoon vanilla extract
- ½ cup Erythritol
- 1 cup plums, pitted, chopped

INGREDIENTS

- 1 cup coconut milk
- 2 cups blueberries

Blueberry Ice Cream

 15 mins 2 h 👤 4

01 Blend the blueberries until you get the smooth puree. Mix blueberry puree with coconut milk.

02 Pour the liquid into the ice cream mold. Freeze the mixture for 1 hour.

03 Stir it well and freeze for an additional hour. Churn the ice cream well before serving.

NUTRITIONAL VALUE	181 calories, 2g protein, 14g carbohydrates, 15g fat, 3g fiber, 9g sugar.

INGREDIENTS

- 1 cup coconut milk
- 1 tablespoon all-purpose flour
- 1 teaspoon vanilla extract
- ⅓ cup Erythritol
- 1 cup raspberries

Coconut and Berries Pudding

 15 mins 40 min 👤 4

01 Bring the coconut milk to a boil and add all-purpose flour. Stir the mixture fast to get the smooth liquid and bring it to a boil.

02 Cool the mixture till it reaches room temperature and pour it into the serving glasses.

03 Blend Erythritol with raspberries until the berries are crushed.

04 Top the coconut milk pudding with raspberries and refrigerate it for 40 minutes.

NUTRITIONAL VALUE	165 calories, 2g protein, 29g carbohydrates, 15g fat, 3g fiber, 4g sugar.

Orange Pie

🕐 15 mins   🍲 40 min   👤 6

INGREDIENTS

- ½ cup orange juice
- 2 tablespoons orange zest
- 1 teaspoon vanilla extract
- 2 eggs, beaten
- ½ cup Erythritol
- 1 teaspoon ground turmeric
- 1 cup all-purpose flour
- 1 teaspoon baking soda

O1   In the mixing bowl, combine orange juice, vanilla extract, Erythritol, ground turmeric, flour, and baking soda.

O2   When the batter is smooth, pour it into the baking mold and top with grated orange zest.

O3   Bake the pie at 355°F for 40 minutes.

O4   Cool the pie well and cut it into servings.

NUTRITIONAL VALUE

112 calories, 4g protein, 39g carbohydrates, 2g fat, 1g fiber, 2g sugar.

Avocado and Chocolate Mousse

🕐 15 mins   🍲 0 min   👤 4

INGREDIENTS

- ⅓ cup cocoa powder
- 2 avocadoes, peeled, pitted, and chopped
- ¼ cup coconut cream
- ¼ cup Erythritol
- 1 teaspoon vanilla extract

O1   Put all ingredients in the food processor and blend until you get a smooth and fluffy mixture.

O2   Transfer the prepared mousse to the serving glasses or store it in the fridge.

NUTRITIONAL VALUE

207 calories, 3g protein, 26g carbohydrates, 19g fat, 8g fiber, 6g sugar.

INGREDIENTS

- 1 egg, beaten
- 1 teaspoon vanilla extract
- 2 bananas, peeled, chopped
- 1 cup all-purpose flour
- 1 teaspoon baking powder
- 1 teaspoon lemon juice

Banana Muffins

 15 mins 25 min 4

O1 Put all ingredients in the food processor and blend until you get a smooth batter.

O2 Fill each muffin mold with banana batter halfway.

O3 Bake the muffins at 355°F for 25 minutes.

NUTRITIONAL VALUE	188 calories, 5g protein, 38g carbohydrates, 2g fat, 2g fiber, 8g sugar.

INGREDIENTS

- 4 bananas, peeled, frozen, and chopped
- 1 tablespoon vanilla extract

Vanilla and Banana Ice Cream

 10 mins 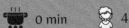 0 min 4

O1 Put frozen bananas and vanilla extract in the food processor. Blend the mixture until smooth.

O2 Transfer the cooked ice cream to the serving bowls.

NUTRITIONAL VALUE	115 calories, 1g protein, 27g carbohydrates, 0g fat, 3g fiber, 15g sugar.

Pomegranate Popsicles

 15 mins   3 h   4

INGREDIENTS

- 1 cup water
- 1 cup pomegranate juice
- ½ cup orange juice

01 Mix all ingredients and pour them into the popsicle molds.

02 Freeze the popsicles for 3 hours.

NUTRITIONAL VALUE

53 calories, 0g protein, 13g carbohydrates, 0g fat, 0g fiber, 11g sugar.

Blackberry Popsicles

🕐 15 mins 🍲 3 h 👤 4

INGREDIENTS

- 1 cup coconut cream
- ½ cup Erythritol
- 2 cups blackberries

01 Blend blackberries with Erythritol until smooth.

02 Mix coconut milk with the blackberry mixture and pour it into the popsicle molds.

03 Freeze the popsicles for 3 hours.

NUTRITIONAL VALUE

170 calories, 2g protein, 23g carbohydrates, 15g fat, 5g fiber, 2g sugar.

INGREDIENTS

- ½ cup quick-cooking oats
- I banana, peeled, mashed
- I egg, beaten
- ¼ cup all-purpose flour
- ½ cup Erythritol
- I teaspoon vanilla extract

Oatmeal Cookies

 15 mins 25 min 4

O1 In the mixing bowl, combine oats with banana, egg, flour, Erythritol, and vanilla extract until homogeneous.

O2 Form the small cookies from the mixture with the help of a spoon.

O3 Place the cookies on the baking sheet and cook them for 25 minutes at 350°F.

NUTRITIONAL VALUE — 113 calories, 4g protein, 50g carbohydrates, 2g fat, 2g fiber, 34g sugar.

INGREDIENTS

- I teaspoon baking soda
- ½ cup orange juice
- I cup all-purpose flour
- I egg, beaten
- I teaspoon vanilla extract
- ⅓ cup Erythritol

Orange Muffins

 15 mins 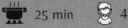 25 min 4

O1 Put all ingredients in the mixing bowl and blend until you get a smooth batter.

O2 Fill each muffin mold with muffin batter halfway and bake the muffins for 25 minutes at 355°F.

NUTRITIONAL VALUE — 148 calories, 5g protein, 27g carbohydrates, 2g fat, 1g fiber, 3g sugar.

60-DAY MEAL PLAN

Approx. 2000 per day calories Diabetes Diet meal plan

DAY	BREAKFAST	LUNCH	SNACK	DINNER
1	Egg and Avocado Toast	Grilled Lemony Salmon Steaks, Quinoa and Spinach Salad, Coconut and Berries Pudding	Tomato Salsa Roasted Paprika Chickpeas	Basil Meatloaf, Garlic and Parsley Red Kidney Beans, Sugar-Free Chocolate Chip Cookies
2	Multigrain Nut Butter Toast	Chicken Gyros, Garden Salad, Apple Pie	Roasted Spicy Pumpkin Seeds	Fragrant Tilapia, Aromatic Couscous, Blueberry Ice Cream
3	Scramble with Avocado	Basil Meatloaf, Arugula Salad, Avocado and Chocolate Mousse	Aromatic Kale Chips, Tomato Salsa	Quinoa and Seeds Bowl, Grilled Thyme Shrimp, Blackberry Popsicles
4	Raspberries Oatmeal	Chicken Stuffed Zucchini, Beetroot Salad, Diabetic Friendly Brownie	Pesto Hummus, Bell Pepper Omelet	Grilled Mahi Mahi Steaks, Cilantro Buckwheat, Orange Muffins
5	Cheese and Zucchini Muffins	Crab Cakes, Watermelon and Mozzarella Salad, Banana Muffins	Roasted Paprika Chickpeas, Cucumber Salad	Paprika and Orange Salmon, Brown Lentils and Carrots Bowl, Plum Tart
6	Low Carb Pancakes with Blackberries	Grilled Pork Strips, Summer Salad, Berries and Oats Muffins	Guacamole, Spiced Roasted Carrot	Teriyaki Chicken, Mushrooms and Buckwheat Bowl, Coconut and Berries Pudding
7	Bell Pepper Omelet	Tuna Salad, Garden Salad, Avocado and Chocolate Mousse	Strawberry and Banana Sorbet, Lemony Artichoke	Lemon and Garlic Chicken Wings, Brown Rice with Pumpkin and Carrot, Sugar-Free Chocolate Chip Cookies
8	Kiwi and Chia Seeds Pudding	Grilled Lemony Salmon Steaks, Zucchini and Pomegranate Salad, Apple Pie	Tomato Salsa, Roasted Spicy Pumpkin Seeds	Chicken and Carrots Sauté, Cilantro Buckwheat, Coconut and Berries Pudding
9	Banana Muffins	Fragrant Tilapia, Spinach and Sweet Potato Bake, Avocado and Chocolate Mousse	Roasted Paprika Chickpeas, Aromatic Kale Chips	Paprika Beef Kabob, Summer Salad, Berries and Oats Muffins
10	Multigrain Nut Butter Toast	Chicken Gyros, Garden Salad, Vanilla and Banana Ice Cream	Roasted Spicy Pumpkin Seeds	Basil Meatloaf, Quinoa and Spinach Salad, Sugar-Free Chocolate Chip Cookies

DAY	BREAKFAST	LUNCH	SNACK	DINNER
11	Egg and Avocado Toast	Grilled Mahi Mahi Steaks, Arugula Salad, Plum Tart	Tomato Salsa Roasted Paprika Chickpeas	Teriyaki Chicken, Brown Rice with Pumpkin and Carrot, Coconut and Berries Pudding
12	Cheese and Zucchini Muffins	Fragrant Tilapia, Cucumber Salad, Blueberry Ice Cream	Pesto Hummus, Aromatic Kale Chips	Chicken Stuffed Zucchini, Mushrooms and Buckwheat Bowl, Orange Muffins
13	Raspberries Oatmeal	Chicken Gyros, Beetroot Salad, Avocado and Chocolate Mousse	Tomato Salsa, Roasted Spicy Pumpkin Seeds	Fragrant Tilapia, Brown Lentils and Carrots Bowl, Sugar-Free Chocolate Chip Cookies
14	Scramble with Avocado	Basil Meatloaf, Arugula Salad, Apple Pie	Roasted Paprika Chickpeas, Lemony Artichoke	Grilled Lemony Salmon Steaks, Cilantro Buckwheat, Diabetic Friendly Brownie
15	Banana Muffins	Fragrant Tilapia, Spinach and Sweet Potato Bake, Avocado and Chocolate Mousse	Roasted Paprika Chickpeas, Aromatic Kale Chips	Paprika Beef Kabob, Summer Salad, Berries and Oats Muffins
16	Multigrain Nut Butter Toast	Chicken Gyros, Garden Salad, Vanilla and Banana Ice Cream	Roasted Spicy Pumpkin Seeds	Basil Meatloaf, Quinoa and Spinach Salad, Sugar-Free Chocolate Chip Cookies
17	Egg and Avocado Toast	Grilled Mahi Mahi Steaks, Arugula Salad, Plum Tart	Tomato Salsa, Roasted Paprika Chickpeas	Teriyaki Chicken, Brown Rice with Pumpkin and Carrot, Coconut and Berries Pudding
18	Cheese and Zucchini Muffins	Fragrant Tilapia, Cucumber Salad, Blueberry Ice Cream	Pesto Hummus, Aromatic Kale Chips	Chicken Stuffed Zucchini, Mushrooms and Buckwheat Bowl, Orange Muffins
19	Raspberries Oatmeal	Chicken Gyros, Beetroot Salad, Avocado and Chocolate Mousse	Tomato Salsa, Roasted Spicy Pumpkin Seeds	Fragrant Tilapia, Brown Lentils and Carrots Bowl, Sugar-Free Chocolate Chip Cookies
20	Scramble with Avocado	Basil Meatloaf, Arugula Salad, Apple Pie	Roasted Paprika Chickpeas, Lemony Artichoke	Grilled Lemony Salmon Steaks, Cilantro Buckwheat, Diabetic Friendly Brownie
21	Banana Muffins	Fragrant Tilapia, Spinach and Sweet Potato Bake, Avocado and Chocolate Mousse	Roasted Paprika Chickpeas, Aromatic Kale Chips	Paprika Beef Kabob, Summer Salad, Berries and Oats Muffins
22	Multigrain Nut Butter Toast	Chicken Gyros, Garden Salad, Vanilla and Banana Ice Cream	Roasted Spicy Pumpkin Seeds	Basil Meatloaf, Quinoa and Spinach Salad, Sugar-Free Chocolate Chip Cookies
23	Egg and Avocado Toast	Grilled Mahi Mahi Steaks, Arugula Salad, Plum Tart	Tomato Salsa Roasted Paprika Chickpeas	Teriyaki Chicken, Brown Rice with Pumpkin and Carrot, Coconut and Berries Pudding

DAY	BREAKFAST	LUNCH	SNACK	DINNER
24	Cheese and Zucchini Muffins	Fragrant Tilapia, Cucumber Salad, Blueberry Ice Cream	Pesto Hummus, Aromatic Kale Chips	Chicken Stuffed Zucchini, Mushrooms and Buckwheat Bowl, Orange Muffins
25	Raspberries Oatmeal	Chicken Gyros, Beetroot Salad, Avocado and Chocolate Mousse	Tomato Salsa, Roasted Spicy Pumpkin Seeds	Fragrant Tilapia, Brown Lentils and Carrots Bowl, Sugar-Free Chocolate Chip Cookies
26	Scramble with Avocado	Basil Meatloaf, Arugula Salad, Apple Pie	Roasted Paprika Chickpeas, Lemony Artichoke	Grilled Lemony Salmon Steaks, Cilantro Buckwheat, Diabetic Friendly Brownie
27	Banana Muffins	Fragrant Tilapia, Spinach and Sweet Potato Bake, Avocado and Chocolate Mousse	Roasted Paprika Chickpeas, Aromatic Kale Chips	Paprika Beef Kabob, Summer Salad, Berries and Oats Muffins
28	Multigrain Nut Butter Toast	Chicken Gyros, Garden Salad, Vanilla and Banana Ice Cream	Roasted Spicy Pumpkin Seeds	Basil Meatloaf, Quinoa and Spinach Salad, Sugar-Free Chocolate Chip Cookies
29	Egg and Avocado Toast	Grilled Mahi Mahi Steaks, Arugula Salad, Plum Tart	Tomato Salsa, Roasted Paprika Chickpeas	Teriyaki Chicken, Brown Rice with Pumpkin and Carrot, Coconut and Berries Pudding
30	Cheese and Zucchini Muffins	Fragrant Tilapia, Cucumber Salad, Blueberry Ice Cream	Pesto Hummus, Aromatic Kale Chips	Chicken Stuffed Zucchini, Mushrooms and Buckwheat Bowl, Orange Muffins
31	Raspberries Oatmeal	Chicken Gyros, Beetroot Salad, Avocado and Chocolate Mousse	Tomato Salsa, Roasted Spicy Pumpkin Seeds	Fragrant Tilapia, Brown Lentils and Carrots Bowl, Sugar-Free Chocolate Chip Cookies
32	Scramble with Avocado	Basil Meatloaf, Arugula Salad, Apple Pie	Roasted Paprika Chickpeas, Lemony Artichoke	Grilled Lemony Salmon Steaks, Diabetic Friendly Brownie
33	Multigrain Nut Butter Toast	Chicken Gyros, Garden Salad, Vanilla and Banana Ice Cream	Roasted Spicy Pumpkin Seeds	Basil Meatloaf, Quinoa and Spinach Salad, Sugar-Free Chocolate Chip Cookies
34	Egg and Avocado Toast	Grilled Mahi Mahi Steaks, Arugula Salad, Plum Tart	Tomato Salsa, Roasted Paprika Chickpeas	Teriyaki Chicken, Brown Rice with Pumpkin and Carrot, Coconut and Berries Pudding
35	Cheese and Zucchini Muffins	Fragrant Tilapia, Cucumber Salad, Blueberry Ice Cream	Pesto Hummus, Aromatic Kale Chips	Chicken Stuffed Zucchini, Mushrooms and Buckwheat Bowl, Orange Muffins
36	Raspberries Oatmeal	Chicken Gyros, Beetroot Salad, Avocado and Chocolate Mousse	Tomato Salsa, Roasted Spicy Pumpkin Seeds	Fragrant Tilapia, Brown Lentils and Carrots Bowl, Sugar-Free Chocolate Chip Cookies

DAY	BREAKFAST	LUNCH	SNACK	DINNER
37	Scramble with Avocado	Basil Meatloaf, Arugula Salad, Apple Pie	Roasted Paprika Chickpeas, Lemony Artichoke	Grilled Lemony Salmon Steaks, Cilantro Buckwheat, Diabetic Friendly Brownie
38	Multigrain Nut Butter Toast	Chicken Gyros, Garden Salad, Vanilla and Banana Ice Cream	Roasted Spicy Pumpkin Seeds	Basil Meatloaf, Quinoa and Spinach Salad, Sugar-Free Chocolate Chip Cookies
39	Egg and Avocado Toast	Grilled Mahi Mahi Steaks, Arugula Salad, Plum Tart	Tomato Salsa, Roasted Paprika Chickpeas	Teriyaki Chicken, Brown Rice with Pumpkin and Carrot, Coconut and Berries Pudding
40	Cheese and Zucchini Muffins	Fragrant Tilapia, Cucumber Salad, Blueberry Ice Cream	Pesto Hummus, Aromatic Kale Chips	Chicken Stuffed Zucchini, Mushrooms and Buckwheat Bowl, Orange Muffins
41	Raspberries Oatmeal	Chicken Gyros, Beetroot Salad, Avocado and Chocolate Mousse	Tomato Salsa, Roasted Spicy Pumpkin Seeds	Fragrant Tilapia, Brown Lentils and Carrots Bowl, Sugar-Free Chocolate Chip Cookies
42	Scramble with Avocado	Basil Meatloaf, Arugula Salad, Apple Pie	Roasted Paprika Chickpeas, Lemony Artichoke	Grilled Lemony Salmon Steaks, Cilantro Buckwheat, Diabetic Friendly Brownie
43	Banana Muffins	Fragrant Tilapia, Spinach and Sweet Potato Bake, Avocado and Chocolate Mousse	Roasted Paprika Chickpeas, Aromatic Kale Chips	Paprika Beef Kabob, Summer Salad, Berries and Oats Muffins
44	Multigrain Nut Butter Toast	Chicken Gyros, Garden Salad, Vanilla and Banana Ice Cream	Roasted Spicy Pumpkin Seeds	Basil Meatloaf, Quinoa and Spinach Salad, Sugar-Free Chocolate Chip Cookies
45	Blueberry Smoothie, Cheese and Zucchini Muffins	Quinoa and Spinach Salad, Grilled Lemony Salmon Steaks	Roasted Paprika Chickpeas	Chicken and Carrots Sauté, Sugar-Free Chocolate Chip Cookies
46	Blueberry Smoothie, Cheese and Zucchini Muffins	Quinoa and Spinach Salad, Grilled Lemony Salmon Steaks	Roasted Paprika Chickpeas	Chicken and Carrots Sauté, Sugar-Free Chocolate Chip Cookies
47	Egg and Avocado Toast	Arugula Salad, Fragrant Tilapia	Aromatic Kale Chips	Basil Meatloaf, Coconut Oatmeal with Walnuts, Diabetic Friendly Brownie
48	Bell Pepper Omelet	Beetroot Salad, Teriyaki Chicken	Roasted Spicy Pumpkin Seeds	Paprika Beef Kabob, Avocado and Chocolate Mousse
49	Raspberries Oatmeal, Tender Cottage Cheese with Raisin and Cinnamon	Cucumber Salad, Lemon and Garlic Chicken Wings	Sweet Potato Bites	Vegetable Sauté, Grilled Thyme Shrimp, Apple Pie

DAY	BREAKFAST	LUNCH	SNACK	DINNER
50	Banana Muffins, Pecan Oatmeal	Garden Salad, Chicken Stuffed Zucchini	Tomato Salsa	Basil Meat Sauce, Brown Rice with Pumpkin and Carrot, Avocado and Chocolate Mousse
51	Asparagus Quiche, Kiwi and Chia Seeds Pudding	Radish Salad, Grilled Pork Strips	Curry Hummus	Mushroom Bake, Fragrant Tilapia, Sugar-Free Chocolate Chip Cookies
52	Cheese and Zucchini Muffins, Blueberry Ice Cream	Watermelon and Mozzarella Salad, Lemony Lobster	Roasted Paprika Chickpeas	Vegetable Sauté, Fragrant Tilapia, Apple Pie
53	Scramble with Avocado, Berries and Oats Muffins	Cherry Tomato Salad, Grilled Mahi Mahi Steaks	Pesto Hummus	Spinach and Sweet Potato Bake, Fragrant Tilapia, Coconut and Berries Pudding
54	Low Carb Pancakes with Blackberries, Coconut Oatmeal with Walnuts	Veggie Salad, Lemon and Garlic Chicken Wings	Guacamole	Mushroom Bake, Fragrant Tilapia, Sugar-Free Chocolate Chip Cookies
55	Multigrain Nut Butter Toast, Vanilla and Banana Ice Cream	Avocado and Chickpea Salad, Grilled Lemony Salmon Steaks	Roasted Spicy Pumpkin Seeds	Basil Meat Sauce, Brown Rice with Pumpkin and Carrot
56	Banana Muffins, Pecan Oatmeal	Quinoa and Spinach Salad, Fragrant Tilapia	Tomato Salsa	Basil Meatloaf, Beetroot Salad, Apple Pie
57	Blueberry Smoothie, Cheese and Zucchini Muffins	Cucumber Salad, Lemon and Garlic Chicken Wings	Sweet Potato Bites	Vegetable Sauté, Fragrant Tilapia, Sugar-Free Chocolate Chip Cookies
58	Egg and Avocado Toast, Kiwi and Chia Seeds Pudding	Arugula Salad, Fragrant Tilapia	Aromatic Kale Chips	Basil Meat Sauce, Brown Rice with Pumpkin and Carrot, Diabetic Friendly Brownie
59	Raspberries Oatmeal, Tender Cottage Cheese with Raisin and Cinnamon	Radish Salad, Lemon and Garlic Chicken Wings	Guacamole	Vegetable Sauté, Fragrant Tilapia, Sugar-Free Chocolate Chip Cookies
60	Multigrain Nut Butter Toast, Vanilla and Banana Ice Cream	Avocado and Chickpea Salad, Grilled Lemony Salmon Steaks	Tomato Salsa	Basil Meat Sauce, Brown Rice with Pumpkin and Carrot, Diabetic Friendly Brownie

MEASUREMENT CONVERSION CHARTS

MEASUREMENT

CUP	OUNCES	MILLILITERS	TABLESPOONS
1/16 CUPS	1/2 OZ	15 ML	1 TBSP
1/8 CUPS	1 OZ	30 ML	3 TBSP
1/4 CUPS	2 OZ	59 ML	4 TBSP
1/3 CUPS	2.5 OZ	79 ML	5.5 TBSP
3/8 CUPS	3 OZ	90 ML	6 TBSP
1/2 CUPS	4 OZ	118 ML	8 TBSP
2/3 CUPS	5 OZ	158 ML	11 TBSP
3/4 CUPS	6 OZ	177 ML	12 TBSP
1 CUPS	8 OZ	240 ML	16 TBSP
2 CUPS	16 OZ	480 ML	32 TBSP
4 CUPS	32 OZ	960 ML	64 TBSP
5 CUPS	40 OZ	1180 ML	80 TBSP
6 CUPS	48 OZ	1420 ML	96 TBSP
8 CUPS	64 OZ	1895 ML	128 TBSP

WEIGHT

IMPERIAL	METRIC
1/2 OZ	15 G
1 OZ	29 G
2 OZ	57 G
3 OZ	85 G
4 OZ	113 G
5 OZ	141 G
6 OZ	170 G
8 OZ	227 G
10 OZ	283 G
12 OZ	340 G
13 OZ	369 G
14 OZ	397 G
15 OZ	425 G
1 LB	453 G

TEMPERATURE

FAHRENHEIT	CELSIUS
100 °F	37 °C
150 °F	65 °C
200 °F	93 °C
250 °F	121 °C
300 °F	150 °C
325 °F	160 °C
350 °F	180 °C
375 °F	190 °C
400 °F	200 °C
425 °F	220 °C
450 °F	230 °C
500 °F	260 °C
525 °F	274 °C
550 °F	288 °C

Disclaimer Notice:
This book is intended to offer general information about the Diabetic Diet. It is not a substitute for professional medical advice, diagnosis, or treatment. Always seek the advice of your physician or another qualified health provider with any questions you may have regarding a medical condition. Never disregard professional medical advice or delay seeking it because of something you have read in this book. If you suspect you have a health problem, consult your healthcare provider immediately. The author assumes no responsibility for any actions taken based on the information contained in this book.

Made in the USA
Columbia, SC
09 November 2024

45922721R00046